100

Things
You
Need to Know

About

Microsoft®
Windows Vista™

Eric Geier

800 East 96th Street,
Indianapolis, Indiana 46240 USA

100 Things You Need to Know About Microsoft® Windows Vista™

ISBN-13: 9780789737274
ISBN-10: 0-7897-3727-2

Library of Congress Cataloging-in-Publication Data:

Geier, Eric, 1984-
  100 things you need to know about Microsoft Windows Vista / Eric
Geier. -- 1st ed.
    p. cm.
  ISBN 0-7897-3727-2
  1. Microsoft Windows (Computer file) 2. Operating systems (Computers)
I. Title. II. Title: One hundred things you need to know about Microsoft
Windows Vista.
  QA76.76.O63G43 2007
  005.4'46--dc22
                          2007036760
Printed in the United States of America
First Printing: November 2007

Trademarks

All terms mentioned in this book that are known to be trademarks or service marks have been appropriately capitalized. Que Publishing cannot attest to the accuracy of this information. Use of a term in this book should not be regarded as affecting the validity of any trademark or service mark.

Warning and Disclaimer

Every effort has been made to make this book as complete and as accurate as possible, but no warranty or fitness is implied. The information provided is on an "as is" basis. The author and the publisher shall have neither liability nor responsibility to any person or entity with respect to any loss or damages arising from the information contained in this book.

Bulk Sales

Que Publishing offers excellent discounts on this book when ordered in quantity for bulk purchases or special sales. For more information, please contact

> **U.S. Corporate and Government Sales**
> **1-800-382-3419**
> **corpsales@pearsontechgroup.com**

For sales outside of the U.S., please contact

> **International Sales**
> **international@pearsoned.com**

This Book Is Safari Enabled

The Safari® Enabled icon on the cover of your favorite technology book means the book is available through Safari Bookshelf. When you buy this book, you get free access to the online edition for 45 days.

Safari Bookshelf is an electronic reference library that lets you easily search thousands of technical books, find code samples, download chapters, and access technical information whenever and wherever you need it.

To gain 45-day Safari Enabled access to this book:

- Go to http://www.quepublishing.com/safarienabled.
- Complete the brief registration form.
- Enter the coupon code DBLA-WVMM-DWGL-WPMV-PVL5.

If you have difficulty registering on Safari Bookshelf or accessing the online edition, please email customer-service@safaribooksonline.com.

Associate Publisher
Greg Wiegand

Acquisitions and Development Editor
Rick Kughen

Managing Editor
Gina Kanouse

Project Editor
Anne Goebel

Copy Editor
Karen Annett

Indexer
Lisa Stumpf

Proofreader
Kathy Ruiz

Technical Editor
Christian Kenyeres

Publishing Coordinator
Cindy Teeters

Designer
Anne Jones

Composition
Nonie Ratcliff

Contents at a Glance

About the Author

Eric Geier is an author of many computing and wireless networking books, including *Geeks on Call PCs: 5-Minute Fixes*, published by John Wiley and Sons and *Wi-Fi Hotspots: Setting Up Public Wireless Internet Access*, published by Cisco Press. Eric also is a regular contributor of tutorials at Wi-FiPlanet.com, an online resource for wireless network administrators and users.

Through spending countless days and nights in front of the computer since he could type and working in the Information Technology (IT) field as an adult, Eric has gained expertise in computers and Microsoft Windows.

For more information about Eric Geier and his writings, visit his website at www.egeier.com.

Dedication

To my wife Sierra, and my daughter Madison, for your motivation and love.

Acknowledgments

I would like to thank everyone who has worked on this book. Working with Que Publishing and Pearson Education has been a great experience!

Special thanks to my mom, Aylsie Geier, for giving periodic feedback on my work.

Thanks to my agent Carole McClendon, from Waterside Productions, for coordinating the pairing of myself and Pearson Education to write this book.

We Want to Hear from You!

As the reader of this book, *you* are our most important critic and commentator. We value your opinion and want to know what we're doing right, what we could do better, what areas you'd like to see us publish in, and any other words of wisdom you're willing to pass our way.

As an associate publisher for Que Publishing, I welcome your comments. You can email or write me directly to let me know what you did or didn't like about this book—as well as what we can do to make our books better.

Please note that I cannot help you with technical problems related to the topic of this book. We do have a User Services group, however, where I will forward specific technical questions related to the book.

When you write, please be sure to include this book's title and author as well as your name, email address, and phone number. I will carefully review your comments and share them with the author and editors who worked on the book.

Email: feedback@quepublishing.com

Mail: Greg Wiegand
         Associate Publisher
         Que Publishing
         800 East 96th Street
         Indianapolis, IN 46240 USA

Reader Services

Visit our website and register this book at www.informit.com/title/9780789737274 for convenient access to any updates, downloads, or errata that might be available for this book.

Introduction

The purpose of this book is to provide you with information, tips, and tricks about using and transitioning to Windows Vista.

Although there are many other books published that discuss Windows Vista, most cover basic tasks (such as printing and opening documents) and are tailored toward those less experienced in computers. If you have experience with computers and Microsoft Windows, you'll find that this book offers better value. Basic tasks and information that you will probably figure out on your own are skipped in this book, and items that you typically wouldn't discover using your computing common sense and previous Windows experience are emphasized.

This book will help you analyze your PC and computer peripherals for their Vista readiness, and discuss upgrading components to achieve better performance. Also covered is how to back up or transfer your files and settings when upgrading a PC or when purchasing a new system. You'll also learn about the different editions of Windows Vista to find which will provide the best fit for your personal, family, or business needs.

After the preparations, you'll be stepped through the Windows installation, and then introduced to the redesigned and enhanced Vista interface and functionality. You'll also learn about the new Windows applications and features. Furthermore, you'll see how to change Vista back to the classic look and feel, find relocated items, and discover many tips and tricks, using simple step-by-step procedures and bullets.

Overall, this book will improve your entire Windows Vista experience!

What's in This Book

This book contains information and steps useful when transitioning to Windows Vista, whether you're upgrading a PC or purchasing a new system loaded with Vista.

Here's a chapter-by-chapter summary:

- **Chapter 1: Upgrading to Windows Vista** shows you how to check if your computer and peripherals are compatible with Windows Vista, and gives tips on common hardware upgrades you might perform and on transferring and backing up your data for the transition to Vista.

- **Chapter 2: Choosing and Installing a Windows Vista Version** helps you understand what each Vista edition provides and steps you through the installation and initial setup of Windows Vista.

- **Chapter 3: Introducing Windows Vista** shows you the new interface of Windows Vista and discusses the main features and applications.

- **Chapter 4: Changing the Look and Feel of Vista** shows step-by-step how to convert the new (and sometimes annoying) Vista desktop and interface to one you'll easily recognize.

- **Chapter 5: Finding Your Way Around in Vista** serves as a reference for finding settings, applications, and features in Vista that have been relocated, or moved from where they resided in Windows XP.

- **Chapter 6: Tips and Tricks** covers customization tasks and neat things to do in Windows Vista.

Who Can Use This Book

This book is intended for PC users, at homes and businesses, who are transitioning to Windows Vista.

This book is tailored toward those with moderate (or at least some) PC and Windows XP experience, such as being able to easily navigate to desired applications and files, perform various settings and preference changes, create shortcuts on the desktop, and uninstall software.

Although experience with Windows XP is suggested, others coming straight from Windows 98 can learn things from this book as well.

How to Use This Book

I hope that this book is easy enough to read that you don't need instructions. That said, there are a few elements that bear explaining.

First, there are several special elements in this book, presented in what we in the publishing business call "margin notes." There are different types of margin notes for different types of information, as you see here.

 NOTE

This is a note that presents information of interest, even if it isn't wholly relevant to the discussion in the main text.

 TIP

This is a tip that might prove useful for whatever it is you're in the process of doing.

 CAUTION

This is a caution, warning you that something you might accidentally do could have undesirable results.

In the book, I give websites to visit (for example, www.microsoft.com) for more information on particular topics or to download something. When you see one of these addresses (also known as a URL), you can go to that web page by entering the URL into the Address bar in your web browser, such as Microsoft Internet Explorer. I've made every effort to ensure the accuracy of the web addresses presented here, but given the ever-changing nature of the web, don't be surprised if you run across an address or two that's changed. I apologize in advance.

Get Ready to Vista!

With all these preliminaries out of the way, it's now time to get started. Although I recommend reading the book in consecutive order, it isn't completely necessary. For example, you might want to skip the first two chapters if you already have Windows Vista installed; or, you might decide that you like Vista's new look, and, therefore, pass by Chapter 4.

So, get ready to turn the page and learn more about Windows Vista. I know you'll discover some neat features and take away loads of information that will improve your Vista experience!

Upgrading to Windows Vista

ant the cool new interface and all the cutting-edge features that Windows Vista offers? Well, before you run out and buy the software for your existing PC, you need to ensure your system will support it!

If you've purchased your PC within the last 2 or 3 years, chances are that Vista will work for you; however, you should make sure before putting down the cash. Furthermore, if it has been more than a few years since you purchased your PC, you should definitely evaluate your system. It might require upgrades or enhancements before using Vista, which this chapter helps you accomplish.

This chapter, along with discussing the use of the automated Upgrade Advisor, shows step-by-step how to manually check whether your PC and other hardware and software are supported for use with Windows Vista. This chapter also gives tips when performing common upgrade tasks—many of which you might need to do before installing Vista.

For those planning to purchase a new PC system preloaded with Vista, rather than upgrading an existing system, you should skip ahead to topics #9 through #11.

1 Use Windows Vista Upgrade Advisor

The first thing to do when thinking about upgrading one of your Windows XP PCs to Windows Vista is to evaluate your PC and its system components to ensure it can be upgraded. Although you can manually review and evaluate your PC against the requirements and recommendations for Vista, as discussed in the next sections, you can make the whole process easier by simply using the Windows Vista Upgrade Advisor. The Windows Vista Upgrade Advisor is a blessing for beginners.

In addition to quickly showing any compatibility issues with your PC's hardware or software, the Windows Vista Upgrade Advisor also tries to come up with solutions to any found issues, and gives recommendations on which Vista version would work best with your system and for your computing needs. The Upgrade Advisor also lets you know if your system will support new, resource-hogging features, such as Vista's Aero interface.

Let's get started by downloading and installing the advisor:

1. Open your web browser and go to the following web page (see Figure 1.1):

    www.microsoft.com/windows/products/windowsvista/buyorupgrade/upgradeadvisor.mspx

TIP

In addition to using the Upgrade Advisor when upgrading from Windows XP, you can also use it with Windows Vista to evaluate your system for an upgrade to a different flavor of Vista.

TIP

If you find that the location of the Upgrade Advisor has changed from the address given in step 1, you can visit the Microsoft Windows main website (www.microsoft.com/windows), browse to the Windows Vista section, and find a link to the Upgrade Advisor.

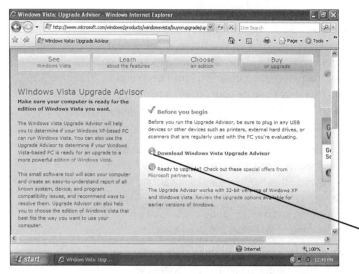

① Click here to download the Windows Vista Upgrade Advisor.

FIGURE 1.1

Example of the Windows Vista Upgrade Advisor web page.

2. Click the Download Windows Vista Upgrade Advisor link to download the program to your computer. The Download Details page will appear.

3. To begin the download, click the Download button.

4. On the File Download–Security Warning prompt, click Save, as shown in Figure 1.2.

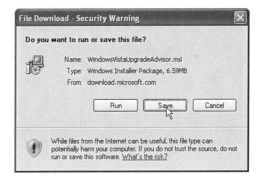

FIGURE 1.2

Saving the Windows Vista Upgrade Advisor to your computer.

5. Browse to and select a location to place the file (Figure 1.3 shows the file being saved to the Desktop), and click Save.

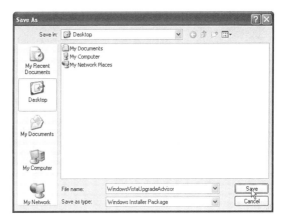

FIGURE 1.3

Saving the Windows Vista Upgrade Advisor files after downloading.

6. After the download is completed, click Run (see Figure 1.4) to begin the installation of the Windows Vista Upgrade Advisor. Microsoft Internet Explorer should display a warning dialog box, asking you to confirm that you want to run this software. Click Run.

FIGURE 1.4

Starting the Windows Vista Upgrade Advisor setup.

7. The Windows Vista Upgrade Advisor Setup Wizard will appear. Click Next (see Figure 1.5).

FIGURE 1.5

The Windows Vista Upgrade Advisor Setup Wizard.

8. Complete the installation by following the directions given by the setup wizard.

 TIP

To get the most out of the Upgrade Advisor, you should make sure all your devices, such as external drives, printers, and scanners, are plugged in and powered on before running the Windows Vista Upgrade Advisor. This allows the Upgrade Advisor to provide feedback on the compatibility of these devices as well.

After the installation is complete, you can run the advisor:

1. Open the Windows Vista Upgrade Advisor by clicking on the icon on the Start menu (see Figure 1.6), or double-click on the desktop icon (if you chose to install it).

(1) Click Start.

(2) Choose All Programs.

(3) Select Windows Vista Upgrade Advisor.

FIGURE 1.6

Opening Windows Vista Upgrade Advisor from the Start menu.

 TIP

If you would like a second opinion about your PC's ability to support Windows Vista, you can check out PC Pitstop's Vista Readiness Center at www.pcpitstop. com/vistaready.

2. Click Start Scan.

   While waiting for the scan to complete, you can compare each flavor of Vista, as shown in Figure 1.7.

3. After the scan is completed, click the See Details button.

4. Now you can review your report. The following pages provide details on using the Upgrade Advisor.

The first thing to look for when viewing your report from the Windows Vista Upgrade Advisor is the message at the top, which will give you a quick, in-a-nutshell idea of your system's compatibility with Windows Vista.

Figure 1.8 shows an example of a recommendation explaining that the system in question might not be well suited to Vista without some upgrades first.

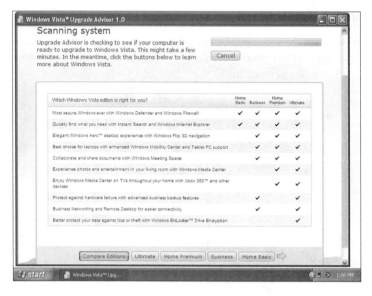

FIGURE 1.7

Buttons to access information about Windows Vista.

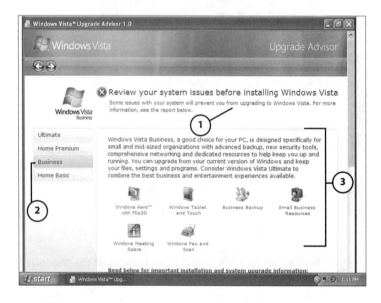

1 Overall advice from Update Advisor

2 Choose a version of Vista here and…

3 …read a description of who is best suited for this version.

FIGURE 1.8

Upgrade Advisor provides an in-a-nutshell summary of your system's prospects with Vista.

The middle part of the report is simply an introduction to the different Vista editions, similar to what was shown while the Upgrade Advisor scanned the system. Use the buttons to the left to choose a version of Vista about which you want to know more.

The bottom of the report (see Figure 1.9) is where you can access more details on any issues that were found during the scan.

(1) Advisor categories

(2) Number of issues found in each category

(3) Click to read more about the identified issues.

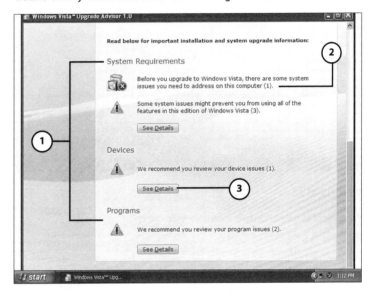

FIGURE 1.9

The bottom of the report is where you can access more details on any found issues.

 TIP

Before closing the report, it's also a good idea to print the task list and save the report, using the buttons in the upper-right corner of the report, so that you can reference the recommendations later.

Clicking on the See Details buttons takes you to the corresponding section of the Report Details page; Figure 1.10 shows the System section of the Report Details page.

On the Report Details page, you can click on the tabs (System, Devices, and Programs) to view the details of the other sections of the report, or you can click on the Task List tab to review the summary of what it recommends you should do before and after the upgrade to Vista.

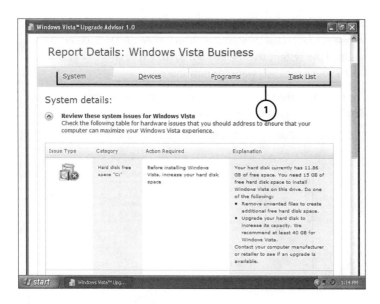

1 Click tabs to scan through the report categories.

FIGURE 1.10

Example of the report's details on the System section.

2 System Requirements and Recommendations

In case you can't get the Windows Vista Upgrade Advisor to work properly on your PC or you want to take a quick look at what it takes to run Windows Vista, this section covers the system requirements and recommendations. In addition, you can refer to the next several sections on how to manually check the specs of the different system components on your PC.

First, you can take a look at the bare-minimum system requirements to install and run Windows Vista:

- 800MHz processor
- 512MB of memory (RAM)
- 20GB hard drive with at least 15GB of available space
- Support for Super VGA graphics
- CD-ROM drive

If you are not familiar with the units of measure for hertz and/or bytes, the following list might help you understand the orders of magnitude:

kB (kilobyte) = 1000 bits

MB (megabyte) = 1,000kB (1,000,000 bits)

GB (gigabyte) = 1,000MB (1,000,000,000 bits)

MHz (megahertz) = 1,000kHz

GHz (gigahertz) = 1,000MHz

For example, 500MB is half of a gigabyte and 3GHz is 3,000 MHz.

This should help when comparing system specifications.

It's important to keep in mind that you won't experience very good performance and won't be able to use many of the neat new features of Vista if running on a system just meeting the bare-minimum requirements. Therefore, you might want to only install and use Windows Vista on a system exceeding the recommended system requirements, as shown in Table 1.1.

Table 1.1 Recommended System Requirements

	Home Basic	Home Premium/ Business/Ultimate
Processor	1GHz (32-bit or 64-bit)	
Memory (RAM)	512MB	1GB
Hard drive	20GB (15+ available)	40GB (15+ available)
Graphics	Support for DirectX 9 graphics with: 32MB of graphics memory	Support for DirectX 9 graphics with: 128MB of graphics memory (minimum) 32 bits per pixel WDDM Driver Pixel Shader 2.0 in hardware
CD drive	DVD-ROM	
Audio output	Recommended	
Internet access	Recommended for Windows activation, updates, and other tasks	

You can use the following sections to manually look up your PC specs, so you can compare them against the requirements and recommendations.

Check the Processor (CPU)

3

The central processor unit (CPU) is the component that's responsible for processing the information and commands between the different components that make up your PC, which basically makes it the brain of your PC. Therefore, the speed of the processor greatly influences your PC's performance. When considering the upgrade to Windows Vista, you need to ensure your CPU can process quickly enough to support the new features of Vista. A sample CPU is shown in Figure 1.11.

FIGURE 1.11

Example of a processor; courtesy of Advanced Micro Devices, Inc.

Here's how to check your processor information in Windows XP:

1. Open the Start menu and click on Control Panel.
2. When in Category View, click the Performance and Maintenance category.

   If in Classic View, simply double-click on the System icon and proceed to step 4.
3. Click on the System icon.
4. Refer to the Computer section, as shown in Figure 1.12.

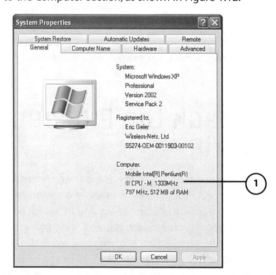

 CPU type and speed are shown here, as well as total RAM.

> 🖳 **TIP**
>
> You can get to the System (and processor) details even quicker if you have the My Computer icon displayed on your desktop: Simply right-click the icon and select Properties.

FIGURE 1.12

Processor and memory configurations are shown in System Properties.

4 Check Memory [RAM]

Along with the processor, the amount of random access memory (RAM), or simply memory for short, greatly influences your PC's performance. Rather than a shortage component like a hard drive, RAM (Figure 1.13 shows an example) is used when the information needs to be quickly read or written, such as temporarily storing information when running software applications.

FIGURE 1.13

Example of computer memory; courtesy of Micron Technology, Inc.

You need to make sure your PC is loaded with adequate memory because Windows Vista requires much more memory than Windows XP. You're probably good to go if you've purchased your system within the last few years; however, if more memory is required or recommended, you can easily add more, which is actually just about the easiest hardware system upgrade you can perform while providing a great enhancement.

To determine how much RAM you have in your system, follow the same steps outlined in #3, "Check the Processor (CPU)." The amount of RAM is shown in the same dialog box showing CPU type and speed.

Here are a few tips if you want to add more memory:

■ Check how many untaken and total memory slots are in your PC by peeking inside your computer.

■ Most PCs have two or three memory slots located on the motherboard in plain sight.

- Check the maximum amount of memory supported for your system by referring to your PC's product documentation or manuals.

- Find memory that's compatible with your specific system, which is also likely found in your PC's documentation or manuals.

- You can use online tools, such as the System Scanner (www. crucial.com/systemscanner), which will scan your system and let you know exactly what memory is compatible with your particular system; using this method eliminates manually inspecting your PC and figuring out all the specifics of your system.

5 Verify Hard Drive Space

As you probably know, all the files and software on your PC take up space on the hard drive (see Figure 1.14), which is the main data storage component in a PC. Hard drives store your email, pictures, movies, music files, letters, work files, and everything else you create, along with thousands of files that comprise the operating system. With each version of the OS, Windows has gotten larger and larger. Vista needs about 10 times more space than Windows XP.

FIGURE 1.14

Example of a hard drive; courtesy of Western Digital Corporation.

Follow these steps in Windows XP to manually check your available disk space:

1. Open My Computer or Windows Explorer.

2. Right-click on the main hard drive and select Properties; Figure 1.15 shows an example.

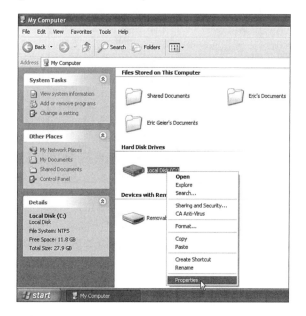

FIGURE 1.15

Accessing the desktop properties.

3. Refer to the Free Space amount, as shown in Figure 1.16.

If you're low (or going to run low after the Vista installation) on disk space, here are a few things you can do to make more room:

■ Organize your personal files and documents and delete any unwanted files.

■ Run the Disk Cleanup utility (which can be found by navigating to Start, All Programs, Accessories, System Tools) to clear the Recycle Bin and temporary files.

■ Uninstall unused or unwanted software applications or games.

■ Consider moving or archiving items that take up a great deal of space to another location, such as a USB flash drive, CDs, DVDs, or a secondary hard drive.

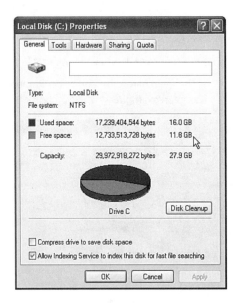

FIGURE 1.16

Checking the available disk space.

If you find that you can't free up enough space, you might have to add another hard drive. Here are some tips to get you started:

- It might be easier to free up room on your existing main hard drive by moving personal files and large applications to the additional hard drive you're installing.

- Consider getting an external hard drive for easier installation and mobility.

- Investigate your PC's connection types, such as if you have USB (and if it's version 1.1 or 2.0) for external drives or whether you have EIDE or SATA for internal drives. USB 2.0 is the best bet. SATA drives are faster.

- You can use online tools, such as InSPECS (www.powerleap.com), which will scan your system and give hardware recommendations that are compatible with your particular system; using this method eliminates manually inspecting your PC and figuring out all the specifics of your system.

6 Check CD Drive Type

You should pay close attention to the type of CD drive your PC has because the retail version of Windows Vista only comes packaged with a DVD rather than a plain CD. Fitting everything for Vista on one DVD rather than having to use multiple CDs is beneficial; however, it's not that uncommon for older PCs—even those sold in the past several years—to not include a DVD drive.

To see if your drive is DVD capable, just look at the front of the drive door. You should see a DVD logo (such as shown in Figure 1.17) along with others, such as the Compact Disc or CD writable/rewritable logos.

FIGURE 1.17

Example of a CD drive with the DVD logos; courtesy of Plextor LLC.

If your PC doesn't have a DVD drive and you prefer not to upgrade your CD drive, you can order a set of plain CDs from Microsoft for a small fee and shipping costs. For more information, visit:

www.microsoft.com/windowsvista/1033/ordermedia

If you're not afraid to open up your PC, you could upgrade your CD drive to a DVD drive, which is fairly easy. It would also save you from having to shell out more money to Microsoft and waiting for the plain CDs in the mail. Here are a few things to consider when switching out your CD drive:

- Although only a regular DVD drive is needed to install Windows Vista, consider purchasing a drive with DVD writing capabilities in case you want to make DVDs in the future.

- Keep in mind the color of the drive if you're concerned about it matching your PC.

- Most PCs have an extra CD drive slot into which you could install the DVD drive, instead of removing the existing CD drive.

7 Verify Graphics Card Specs

If your PC is a few years old (or newer), the graphics card (see Figure 1.18 for an example) will most likely be compatible with all the Windows Vista editions; however, you should check just to make sure. The only item you should be worried about looking up (from the Graphics section of Table 1.1, shown earlier) is the amount of graphics memory, as the other items should be up to spec if the memory requirement is satisfied.

FIGURE 1.18

Example of a graphics card; courtesy of Micron Technology, Inc.

Here's how to check the graphics memory in Windows XP:

1. Right-click on the desktop and select Properties.

2. Select the Settings tab.

3. Click the Advanced button.

4. Select the Adapter tab.

5. Refer to the Memory Size, as shown in Figure 1.19.

If the graphics card isn't up to spec, you can upgrade:

- Along with the specifications mentioned earlier in Table 1.1, consider other optional features, such as High-Definition (HD) capabilities, TV in/out, and S-video outputs.

- Investigate your PC's connection types, such as if you have AGP, PCI, or PCI Express.

■ You can use online tools, such as InSPECS (www.powerleap.com), which will scan your system and give hardware recommendations that are compatible with your particular system; using this method eliminates manually inspecting your PC and figuring out all the specifics of your system.

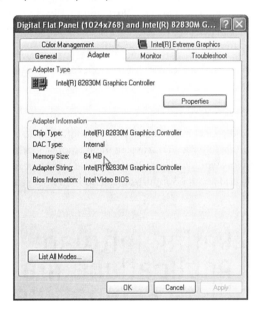

FIGURE 1.19

Checking the amount of graphics memory.

⑧ Verify Audio Card

Because Microsoft doesn't offer many up-front details on the requirements for the audio component, you can either wait until you install Windows Vista to see if the audio works or you can check ahead of time on the Microsoft list of supported components at the following website:

http://winqual.microsoft.com/hcl/

Of course, I recommend that you check first so that you know what to expect when you install Vista.

9 Check PC Peripherals and Accessories

Whether you are upgrading an existing PC or you're planning to purchase a new system preloaded with Vista, you should check that your accessories and/or peripherals (such as printers, scanners, network adapters, and music players) will work with Windows Vista.

First, you can check the Microsoft list of supported components at the following website:

http://winqual.microsoft.com/hcl/

If you can't find your component on the Microsoft list, you can check with the manufacturer/vendor, as some might supply alternative drivers that will work with Windows Vista. Go to the manufacturer's/vendor's website and find the support/download section to search for the device driver.

10 Verify Software Applications Are Vista Compatible

Whether you are upgrading an existing PC or you're planning to purchase a new system preloaded with Vista, you should check that your software applications will be supported with Windows Vista.

You can reference the following lists that Microsoft supplies to see if your applications are supported:

Certified for Windows Vista:

https://winqual.microsoft.com/member/softwarelogo/certifiedlist.aspx

Works with Windows Vista:

https://winqual.microsoft.com/member/softwarelogo/workswithlist.aspx

If the application isn't listed, you can also check the publisher's/vendor's website for information on the product's Windows compatibility before giving up.

11 Move to a New PC Preloaded with Windows Vista

Although buying a new PC system loaded with Windows Vista might have saved you time, you'll probably still need to transfer your files and documents from your old PC to the new one and install your desired software applications.

You can manually round up and transfer your personal files and documents using an external separate hard drive, USB flash drive, or network sharing. Another way to transfer files from an XP computer to your new Vista computer is to use Windows Easy Transfer, which automates the transfer.

Windows Easy Transfer also helps transfer other items such as user accounts, email messages, contacts, and other settings that aren't easy or possible to do manually. Moreover, you can also download and use the Windows Easy Transfer Companion, which can transfer many of your software applications. This saves a great deal of time and the headache of reinstalling all of them.

To download Windows Easy Transfer and Windows Easy Transfer Companion, visit www.microsoft.com/downloads.

After being installed, the Windows Easy Transfer and Windows Easy Transfer Companion utilities can be accessed from the Start menu, as shown in Figure 1.20.

① Click here to open Windows Easy Transfer Companion.

② Click here to open Windows Easy Transfer.

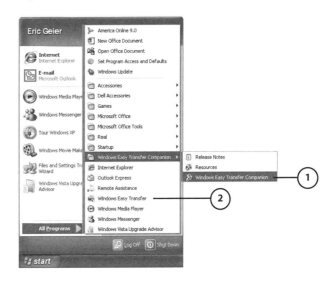

FIGURE 1.20

Accessing the Windows Easy Transfer utilities.

Follow these basic steps when using Windows Easy Transfer to transfer your files and settings:

1. After you open Windows Easy Transfer, you'll see the welcome screen that describes its functionality. Click Next to proceed.

2. You then need to choose and configure your desired transfer method by following the directions in the application and referring to the following:

   ■ **Use an Easy Transfer Cable:** This method uses a special USB cable (typically 8 feet long), which you connect to each computer, to transfer your files and settings in real time. Although you'll need to purchase the cable for around $40, this method provides the quickest transfer speed, using USB 2.0 at 480Mbps, and is typically the easiest option.

   ■ **Transfer directly, using a network connection:** This method uses a network connection between the PCs, which can be on a (wireless or wired) network or via a computer-to-computer (ad hoc) connection. The transfer can be made directly (in real time) or you can copy the data to another PC or network storage device and then transfer the data to your new computer.

   Transferring via a network connection will take longer (around 100Mbps for wired and 25Mbps for wireless) than using the Easy Transfer method. However, if you have an existing network connection between the computers, this method doesn't require any additional investment.

   ■ **Use a CD, DVD, or other removable media:** This method involves copying your data to removable media and then transferring the data to your new computer.

   The transfer speeds vary depending upon the type of media you choose; however, they are typically faster than network connections.

3. After you choose and configure the transfer method, you need to specify what to transfer by following the directions in the application and referring to the following:

   ■ **All User Accounts, Files, and Settings:** Of course, this option transfers all user accounts, files, and settings, but keep in mind this doesn't include items outside of user account areas.

➡ NOTE

User account areas are locations such as My Documents and files and folders located on your desktop. Items not in account areas include files and folders such as on your hard drive's root (for example, C:/folder) or C:/Program Files.

- **My User Account, Files, and Settings Only**: This option transfers the user account, files, and settings for the account you're logged into. Again, keep in mind this doesn't include items outside of user account areas.

- **Advanced Options**: This option automatically selects to transfer all user accounts, files, and settings. However, you can modify exactly what is transferred and this option allows you to add other files and folders not in the user account areas.

4. To begin the backup, click Transfer.

If you used an indirect method of transfer (using removable media or moved data to a networked PC or drive), you'll need to restore your files and settings to your new computer:

1. Copy or move the backup file, by default named SaveData.mig, to your computer.

2. Double-click on the backup file to open it.

3. Click Browse to browse to and select the backup file. If you created a password, enter it in the Password field.

4. Click Next.

5. Review the backup contents and click Transfer to begin.

If you prefer, you can also transfer your applications and software using the Windows Easy Transfer Companion:

1. After you open the Windows Easy Transfer Companion, you'll see the welcome screen that describes its functionality. Click Start to proceed.

2. You then need to choose and configure your desired transfer method by following the directions in the application and referring to the following:

- **Use an Easy Transfer Cable**: This method uses a special USB cable (typically 8 feet long), which you connect to each computer, to transfer your files and settings in real time. Although you'll need to purchase the cable for around $40, this method provides the quickest transfer speed, using USB 2.0 at 480Mbps, and is typically the easiest option.

- **Transfer directly, using a network connection:** This method uses a network connection between the PCs, which can be on a (wireless or wired) network or via a computer-to-computer (ad hoc) connection. Unlike with transferring your files and settings, this utility only supports direct (real-time) transfers.

  Transferring via a network connection will take longer (around 100Mbps for wired and 25Mbps for wireless) than using the Easy Transfer method. However, if you have an existing network connection between the computers, this method doesn't require any additional investment.

3. After you choose and configure the transfer method and both computers perform a scan, a list of applications will be displayed. Specify the applications you want to transfer, and click Next to proceed with the process.

2

Choosing and Installing a Windows Vista Edition

Unlike previous versions of Windows, which came in one or two basic flavors, Vista comes in a whopping five flavors—each offering different features and an entirely different price tag. As you can imagine, making this choice can be daunting. This chapter, however, will help you decide which version is right for you. Regardless of whether you are upgrading an existing computer to Vista or shopping for a new computer with Vista preloaded, this chapter will help you make the best choice.

12 Compare Vista Editions

As you might have already discovered, there are five different editions of Windows Vista you can choose from, which are summarized in the following list:

- **Home Basic**: Includes only the new basic features and is best for light home use on PCs meeting only the minimal system specs.

- **Home Premium**: Allows home/small-office PC users to take advantage of new effects and enhancements to the desktop and special mobility and entertainment features. This edition is best suited for newer PCs that exceed minimum system specs and for those users who use their computers daily.

- **Business**: Comes with better backup and restore features than home editions; however, instead of the entertainment applications, it includes more business applications, such as Remote Desktop Connection and Windows Fax and Scan.

- **Ultimate**: For power users in homes and businesses, this edition provides even better data protection tools and desktop enhancements. This edition is a good choice for those wanting the business features without sacrificing the entertainment applications.

- **Enterprise:** Includes additional tools and features specifically for large businesses with complex computer and technology systems. This edition of Vista isn't realistically available to consumers; it's only available to Volume License customers who have PCs covered by Microsoft Software Assurance.

Table 2.1 gives you a better comparison of the particular features between the four editions available for consumers.

 TIP

The prices shown in Table 2.1 are the suggested retail prices in US dollars. With some searching on the Internet, you can find much lower prices.

Table 2.1 Recommended System Requirements

	Home Basic	Home Premium	Business	Ultimate
Full price	$199.00	$239.00	$299.00	$399.00
Upgrade price	$99.95	$159.00	$199.00	$259.00
Safer for families with Parental Controls	✓	✓	✓	✓
Better security with Windows Defender and Windows Firewall	✓	✓	✓	✓
New and improved user-friendly Network and Sharing Center	✓	✓	✓	✓

	Home Basic	Home Premium	Business	Ultimate
New searching tools with Instant Search and Microsoft Internet Explorer 7	✓	✓	✓	✓
Organize and display pictures with Photo Gallery	✓	✓	✓	✓
Enhanced appearance and live thumbnails with Windows Aero and Flip 3D		✓	✓	✓
Laptop/notebook features with Windows Mobility Center and Tablet PC support		✓	✓	✓
Ability to connect, communicate, and share with others using Windows Meeting Space		✓	✓	✓
Support for multiple displays/monitors with Windows SideShow		✓	✓	✓
Easy backup of files and data with Windows Automatic Backup	✓	✓		
Easy backup of files, data, applications, and operating system with Windows Complete PC Backup and Restore			✓	✓
Advanced sharing and display of media with Windows Media Center		✓		✓
Create DVDs with Windows DVD Maker		✓		✓
Create high definition (HD) movies with Windows Movie Maker		✓		✓
Have fun with new premium games: Chess Titans, Mahjong Titans, and Inkball		✓		✓
Play poker with a Windows Ultimate Extra: Windows Hold'em				✓
Windows Fax and Scan			✓	✓
Remote Desktop Connection			✓	✓
Ability to restore previous versions of documents with Shadow Copy			✓	✓
Enhanced desktop background with full-motion video with Windows DreamScene				✓
Protects data on lost/stolen hard drives with Windows BitLocker Drive Encryption and Secure Online Key Backup				✓
Use multiple languages on a single PC with Language packs				✓

For more information on the specific features from Table 2.1, refer to Chapter 3, "Introducing Windows Vista."

13 Full or Upgrade Version?

As shown in Table 2.1, the upgrade versions of the Windows Vista editions are about $100 cheaper than the full versions. You can use the upgrade versions if you're going to install it on a PC currently running Windows 2000 or Windows XP. PCs with other operating systems (such as Windows 95, 98, or Me), however, don't qualify for an upgrade and a full version of Vista is required.

14 Upgrade In-Place or Clean Install?

If you're planning to use an upgrade version of Windows Vista (see #13, "Full or Upgrade Version?"), you should determine whether you can perform an upgrade in-place installation or if you have to do a clean install installation. This will help you figure out what type of preparation you need to do before installing Windows Vista and might also influence which edition you choose.

If using a full version of Windows Vista (see #13), you'll have to do the clean install installation.

An upgrade in-place installation is typically easier and technically better because it will keep all your existing software applications, files, and settings, whereas the clean install won't. Nevertheless, you may experience problems during the upgrade in-place installation of Windows Vista and loose all your data. You may also have issues down the road because your PC didn't have a fresh start when you installed Vista. Therefore, you should spend a bit more time thoroughly backing up your data (discussed in the next section) before proceeding with either installation method.

You can reference Table 2.2 to see if you're eligible for the upgrade in-place, based on your current Windows version and your desired Vista edition.

 TIP

If you have more than one PC on which you want to install Windows Vista, you might be able to purchase additional licenses (after buying your first Windows Vista package), which are a bit cheaper than buying another full Windows Vista package.

For more information, visit the Microsoft website at:

www.microsoft.com/ windows/products/ windowsvista/ buyorupgrade/addlicense

Table 2.2 Determining the Installation Type

Your Current Windows Version	Home Basic	Home Premium	Business	Ultimate
Windows XP Home	In-place	In-place	In-place	In-place
Windows XP Professional	Clean	Clean	In-place	In-place
Windows XP Professional x64	Clean	Clean	Clean	Clean
Windows 2000	Clean	Clean	Clean	Clean

Column header span: The Version of Vista You've Purchased

For example, if your PC is loaded with Windows XP Home Edition, you could do an in-place installation with any of the four Vista upgrade editions.

You should now have enough information about Windows Vista to make a decision on which edition and version (or possibly additional licenses) to buy.

15 Back Up Your Data

Before installing Windows Vista, you should back up your files, settings, and software applications. This is especially necessary when doing the clean install as it wipes out all your data. As discussed in the previous section, the upgrade in-place installation will keep your data but you should safeguard your information just in case you have problems.

You can manually round up your personal files and documents and put them on a separate hard drive, USB flash drive, CD, DVD, or other form of removable media. Or, you can use Windows Easy Transfer to assist in the backup process if you're using Windows 2000 or XP.

Windows Easy Transfer only backs up your files and settings, therefore you'll have to reinstall your applications after the Windows Vista installation. You should round up your installation disks or the download information and product keys before proceeding with the installation. To download Windows Easy Transfer, visit www.microsoft.com/downloads.

After being installed, the Windows Easy Transfer utility can be accessed from the Start menu, as shown in Figure 2.1.

① Choose Start.

② Select Windows Easy Transfer.

FIGURE 2.1

Accessing Windows Easy Transfer.

Follow these basic steps when using Windows Easy Transfer to back up your files and settings:

1. After you open Windows Easy Transfer, you'll see the welcome screen that describes its functionality. Click Next to proceed.

2. You then need to choose and configure your desired transfer method by following the directions in the application and referring to the following:

   ■ **Use an Easy Transfer Cable:** This method isn't practical for this situation as it transfers the data in real-time.

   ■ **Transfer directly, using a network connection:** This method allows you to back up your data to another PC or network storage device. Then, after you install Windows Vista you can transfer the data back to the computer.

   The transfer speeds vary between the network connection types and your particular equipment and setup; however, you can typically achieve around 100Mbps for wired connections and 25Mbps for wireless connections.

■ **Use a CD, DVD, or other removable media:** This method involves backing up your data to a removable media and then loading the data back onto the computer after the Windows Vista installation.

The transfer speeds vary depending upon the type of media you choose; however, they are typically faster than network connections.

3. After you choose and configure the transfer method, you need to specify what to back up by following the directions in the application and referring to the following:

■ **All User Accounts, Files, and Settings:** Of course, this option transfers all user accounts, files, and settings, but keep in mind this doesn't include items outside of user account areas.

■ **My User Account, Files, and Settings Only:** This option transfers the user account, files, and settings for the account you're logged into. Again, keep in mind this doesn't include items outside of user account areas.

■ **Advanced option:** This option automatically selects to transfer all user accounts, files, and settings. However, you can modify exactly what is transferred and it allows you to add other files and folders that are not in the user account areas.

4. To begin the backup, click Transfer.

 NOTE

User account areas are locations such as My Documents and files and folders located on your desktop. Items not in account areas would be files and folders such as on your hard drive's root (for example, C:/folder) or C:/Program Files.

After you install Windows Vista, you can restore your files and settings:

1. Copy or move the backup file, by default named SaveData.mig, to your computer.

2. Double-click on the backup file to open it.

3. Click Browse to browse to and select the backup file. If you created a password, enter it in the Password field.

4. Click Next.

5. Review the backup contents and click Transfer to begin.

16 Install Windows Vista

Despite the confusion of all the Vista editions and installation methods, Windows Vista is one of the easiest Windows systems to install (after you get the version you're going to use picked out and your data backed up). Simply inserting the DVD will get you started on the approximate 45-minute installation. The following will step you through the process:

1. Log on to your current Windows (or other operating system) and insert the Windows Vista DVD (or specially ordered CD). The DVD should be automatically detected and the Install Now screen will appear (see Figure 2.2).

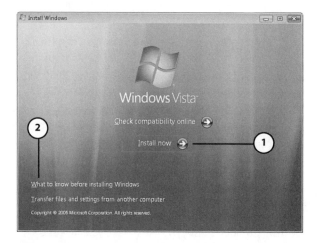

① Click here to install Vista.

② Click here to learn more about Vista.

FIGURE 2.2

Windows Vista installation install screen.

2. Click Install Now. The product key screen (see Figure 2.3) appears.

Windows Vista by default must be activated within 30 days (online or by telephone) or it will stop working. The product activation basically informs Microsoft that the particular product key is being used so they can track additional installations and control software piracy.

Checking the Automatically Activate Windows When I'm Online option will configure Windows to automatically try activating itself three days after your first logon, which is useful because you probably won't have to bother with it again.

 TIP

If Windows does not automatically detect the DVD, you need to manually run the setup program: Click Start, click Run, click Browse, find and select the setup.exe file from the DVD, click OK to return to the Run prompt, and then click OK to run the setup program file.

1. Enter the product key here (you do not need to include the dashes).

2. Check this box to automatically activate your copy of Vista the next time you connect to the Internet.

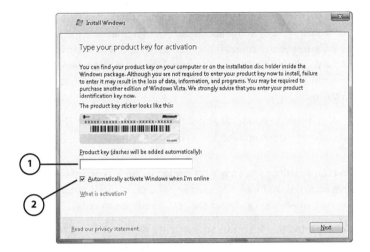

FIGURE 2.3

Windows Vista installation product key screen.

3. If the updates screen (see Figure 2.4) appears, choose an option to continue.

1. Click here to launch Windows Update and download updates that have been added since Vista was released.

2. Click here to skip the updates (though you should update Vista as soon as you get it installed if you skip it here).

3. Click here to send anonymous information to Microsoft to help Microsoft improve the installation process.

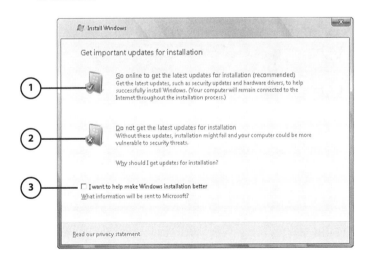

FIGURE 2.4

Windows Vista installation updates screen.

It's best to get the Windows updates now in case you don't remember to do so later. The updates contain fixes and patches that address found bugs, issues, and security holes.

Checking the I Want to Help Make Windows Installation Better option will securely share information about your installation experience (such as any errors you encounter) and PC specifications to Microsoft. It's part of the Windows Installation Customer Experience Improvement Program. For more information, click the What Information Will Be Sent to Microsoft? link.

TIP

To return to the previous window during the setup, you can click the back arrow in the upper-right corner.

4. Type your product key into the field and click Next. The license terms screen appears.

You can actually try out any Vista edition regardless of the one you purchased. Just don't input a product key and click Next. Then, a window appears where you can select the desired edition to install.

Keep in mind that you must activate Vista within 30 days after the installation by inputting a product key matching the installed Vista edition.

5. Review the terms, check the I Accept the License Terms option, and click Next. The installation type screen (see Figure 2.5) appears.

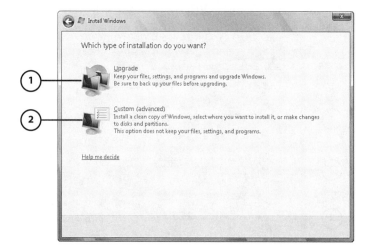

1. Choose Upgrade to perform an in-place installation.

2. Choose Custom (Advanced) to perform a clean install.

FIGURE 2.5

Windows Vista installation type screen.

6. Choose the appropriate type of installation, considering the recommendations discussed earlier in #14, "Upgrade In-Place or Clean Install?" To perform an in-place installation, select Upgrade. To perform a clean installation, choose Custom (Advanced).

7. If you select Custom (Advanced), you will see a screen on which you are asked to choose which hard disk or partition you want to install Vista (see Figure 2.6).

Select where you want to install Windows Vista (and make any desired changes to your drives and partitions) and click Next.

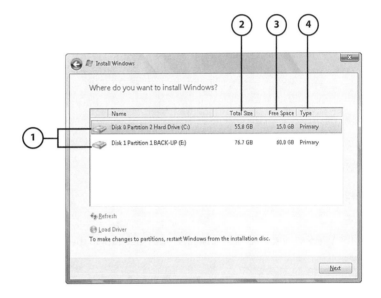

① Drives/partitions on which Vista could be installed (your options will look different depending on the number of drives installed and number of partitions on those drives)

② Total size of the drive or partition

③ Free space on a drive or partition

④ Type of partition

FIGURE 2.6

Windows Vista Installation drive selection and configuration screen.

From this screen, you can make configuration changes to hard drives and partitions. For example, if you're doing a clean install or have properly backed up your data, you can reformat your hard drive(s) which can help eliminate any current or future disk errors.

To access these drive options, you must start the Windows Vista installation from bootup: Exit the installation and with the installation DVD in the drive, restart the computer, and, if prompted, hit a key after the initial boot to load from CD.

After you're back on the drive and partition screen, click the Drive options (Advanced) link to access the tools. Then, use the buttons to perform the configurations. For example, click on a partition and hit Format to reformat the drive/partition.

8. After you're done choosing and/or setting up partitions, click Next to continue. The installation will begin, as shown in Figure 2.7.

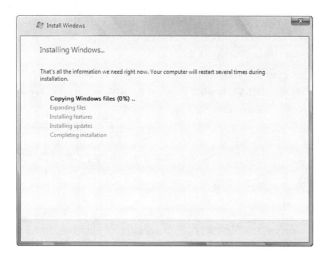

FIGURE 2.7

Beginning the Windows Vista installation.

After Windows Vista has been installed, you'll need to do the initial setup:

1. First, you're prompted (see Figure 2.8) to create a user account. Type a user name and, if desired, a password, and click Next.

 TIP

Using a password helps protects your user account (and your PC) from unauthorized use by other family members and peers. If you have young children, using a password can also help prevent children from altering parental controls settings or making system changes.

FIGURE 2.8

Creating a user account during the Windows Vista installation.

TIP

The computer name is what the PC will be identified by when part of a network, such as when sharing files or printers on your wireless home network.

2. Next you're prompted (see Figure 2.9) to define the computer name and desktop background. Type a computer name and, if desired, select a desktop background, and click Next.

FIGURE 2.9

Defining the computer name and desktop background during the Windows Vista installation.

 NOTE

Remember, you must be connected to the Internet (such as via DSL, cable modem, or a network connection) to download and install the updates.

3. Next you're prompted (see Figure 2.10) to specify whether to download and install updates for Windows Vista. This setting enables or disables Windows Update. It does not install updates during the Vista installation process (you were prompted to do that earlier in the installation process). Choose a desired option and click Next.

4. Next you're prompted (see Figure 2.11) to review/set the time and date settings. If needed, select the correct settings and click Next.

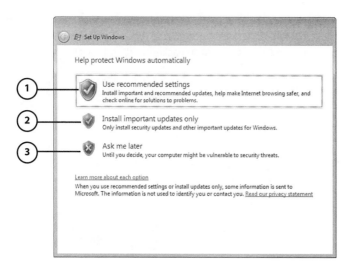

(1) Installs virtually every Windows update, including some you might not want

(2) Installs only crucial updates

(3) Disables Windows Update

FIGURE 2.10

Specifying whether to download and install updates during the Windows Vista installation.

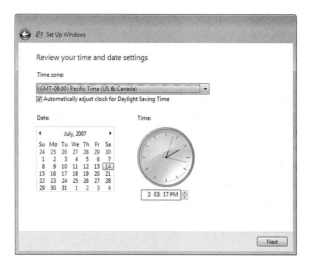

FIGURE 2.11

Reviewing and setting the time and date settings during the Windows Vista installation.

5. If the PC is connected to a network, you're prompted (see Figure 2.12) to specify its type/location. See #20, "Network and Sharing Center," for more information.

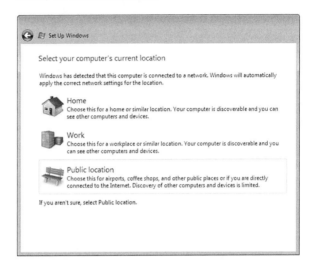

FIGURE 2.12

Specifying a network's type/location during the Windows Vista installation.

6. After you're completely done, you'll see the Thank You screen. Click Start to begin using Vista.

3

Introducing
Windows Vista

In this chapter, you'll discover the new interface and features of Vista. As you'll soon see, Windows Vista is quite a change from the old XP!

I'll break down the key new Vista features and show you which flavor of Vista includes which features. Then, I'll show you how to access each of these new features. If you are a longtime Windows user, you might be tempted to give this chapter short shrift—or skip it altogether—but if you want to get the most enjoyment out of your new operating system, I strongly urge you to keep reading.

17 New Look and Functionality

No matter which Windows Vista edition you choose, or have chosen, it will contain a redesigned look and functionality. The taskbar, Start menu, and the new desktop feature, called Windows Sidebar, will likely be the first noticeable changes you'll discover in Vista.

Figure 3.1 shows examples of the new taskbar, Start menu, and Windows Sidebar.

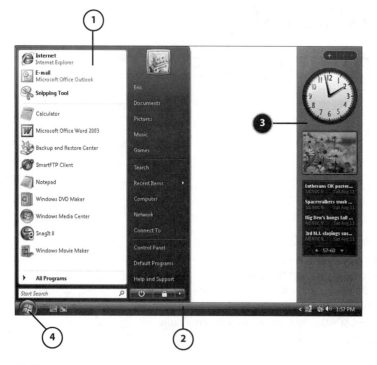

(1) Redesigned Start menu

(2) Taskbar with the new Vista shiny black color scheme

(3) New Windows Sidebar feature

(4) Start button

FIGURE 3.1

New interface and look in Windows Vista.

Taskbar

Longtime Windows users might remember the drastic change in the look and feel of Windows between Windows 95/98 and XP. Microsoft has again changed the scheme in Vista. Gone is the default blue-and-green color scheme XP users know so well. In Windows Vista, Microsoft has chosen a fading black color scheme. Although this tones down the look and brightness of Windows, the black scheme projects a sleek interface.

Another major change to the taskbar is the Start button. The usual button containing the word *start* has been replaced with a Windows logo, which you can see in Figure 3.1.

If your system is capable of running the new Aero interface, Vista offers the use of live thumbnails, which provide a preview of the open document or application, simply by hovering your mouse over an application in the taskbar (see Figure 3.2).

(1) Hovering your mouse over an application in the taskbar…

(2) …shows a live preview, making it easier to determine the contents of each open file.

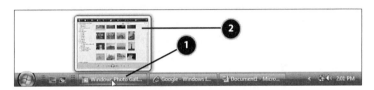

FIGURE 3.2

Example of the taskbar live thumbnails.

The time is still displayed by default on the taskbar in the lower-right corner of the screen. After clicking on the time to bring up the calendar and clock (see Figure 3.3), you'll see that Microsoft has revamped the clock and calendar.

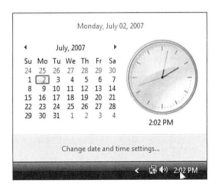

FIGURE 3.3

Calendar and clock in Windows Vista.

> **NOTE**
>
> You might also notice that you can't change the time and date settings as easily as you could in other versions of Windows. You can, however, now set up additional clocks for other time zones or use the military (24-hour) time format if you desire. For more information, see #77, "Set Up Additional Clocks for Other Time Zones," and #78, "Use Military Time Format for the Clock."

Start Menu

As you can see from the example in Figure 3.1, the Start menu now contains a Search box for the new Instant Search feature. Instant Search allows you to quickly find files, programs, email messages, web favorites and history, and more. For more information, see #81, "Search from the Start Menu."

If you are a fan of the Run prompt from previous versions of Windows, you might be disappointed because it's not included on the Start menu by default. You can, however, use the Search box to run commands like you would with the Run applet found in other versions of Windows. Nevertheless, the Run prompt can be accessed in the Accessories section of the Start menu (see Figure 3.4) and can also be added back onto the Start menu if you choose. For more information, see #62, "Run Prompt."

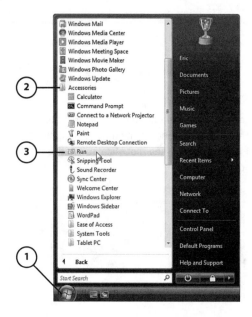

1. Click Start.

2. Choose Accessories.

3. Select Run.

FIGURE 3.4

Run's new location on the Start menu.

Another notable change you'll discover after seeing the Start menu is that the word *My* has been dropped from the names of common items and directories. For example, "My Computer" is now simply "Computer" and "My Network Places" is just "Network." In addition, the My Documents folder is now named after the Windows user. Changes to My Documents are detailed in #51, "My Documents."

 TIP

You can also add these icons (such as Computer and Network) to your desktop. For more information, see #40, "Add the Main Icons."

TIP

Keep in mind that the Lock feature doesn't provide any security if your Windows account isn't password protected! To create and edit account passwords, open User Accounts from Control Panel. Be sure to create a strong password containing both numbers and letters and at least one uppercase letter. Also, don't use easily guessed passwords, such as the names of children or pets. Lastly, don't share your password with anyone.

You'll also likely notice the Turn Off Computer and Log Off buttons have been removed and replaced with other options. The first button on the left, indicated by the power symbol, will put the PC into Sleep mode. Similar to Stand By mode in previous versions of Windows, Sleep mode powers down most of the PC and puts the session into memory so you can resume right where you left off.

The button with the lock will, of course, lock your PC. This option is best used when you want to secure your PC when leaving for short durations. To resume use of the PC, you must press Ctrl+Alt+Delete and enter the Windows account password.

Finally, the other shutdown options are accessible when hovering over the arrow on the right. Figure 3.5 shows an example.

Along with the Sleep and Lock options, this menu also provides the following: Switch User, Log Off, Restart, and Shut Down. These are straightforward, with the exception of Switch User. The Switch User option keeps the current Windows account active when opening another user account, whereas Log Off doesn't. When you switch from one user account to another, you will be prompted for a username and password on each. This is useful if several users need access to the same computer quickly, such as in a business environment.

(1) Enable Sleep mode.

(2) Lock your PC.

(3) Click here for power options.

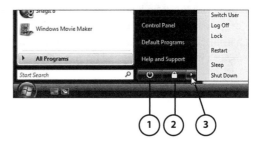

FIGURE 3.5

New location for the power options in Windows Vista.

 TIP

You can change the Power button on the Start menu. See #76, "Change Power Button on Start Menu."

After you click on All Programs, you'll notice a big difference. Rather than the menus branching (opening in fly-out menus), they stay contained in the Start menu.

In addition, it now takes a click rather than just a hover to open the Start menu sections. The scrollbar can be used to browse through the items.

Desktop

Other than the slightly larger default icon size (Figure 3.6 shows an example), not much has changed with the actual desktop.

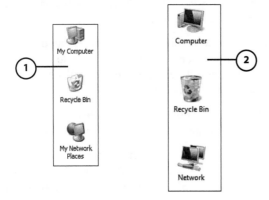

① Icons in Windows XP

② Icons in Windows Vista

FIGURE 3.6

Comparison of Windows XP and Vista default icons.

If you're used to having the main icons (such as My Computer and My Network Places) on your desktop, you can easily add them. See #40, "Add the Main Icons," for more information. Remember that these items have been renamed, with the *My* dropped from the name.

Windows Sidebar

Windows Sidebar is a time- and space-saving program that can be displayed on the side of your screen, as shown earlier in Figure 3.1. Windows Sidebar contains your desired gadgets that display and provide accessibility to certain things. Examples of gadgets include personalized slideshows of your photos, news and weather feeds, quick access to contacts and notes, and much more.

For more information on how to use Windows Sidebar, see #75, "Add More Gadgets to Sidebar."

18 Parental Controls

The parental controls in Vista significantly surpass those in earlier versions of Windows, which only provided website-filtering capabilities with the Content Advisor in Microsoft Internet Explorer. In addition to improved website filtering, Windows Vista allows you to control and monitor the usage of the computer, applications, games, email, and instant messaging. Finally, you can take control of just about anything your children do on a computer, without the need for third-party software.

Controlling Capabilities

Vista's parental controls are a far cry better than those found in XP:

- Windows Vista web filter
  - Allows you to use automatic web content filtering options, including High, Medium, None, and Custom. Choosing Custom allows you to filter based upon desired categories such as Drugs, Tobacco, Pornography, and Bomb Making.
  - Allows you to block certain websites and provides options to override automatic web content filtering options if the user is on the allow list.
  - Allows you to block file downloads.
- Time limits
  - Allows you to specify exactly (hour by hour) when the user can be logged on to the computer
- Games
  - Allows you to specify whether the user can play games
  - Allows you to block or allow games by ratings (such as Everyone, Teen, and Mature) and content types (such as Crude Humor, Blood, Language, and Online Games)
  - Allows you to block or allow specific games, regardless of its rating
- Allow and block specific programs
  - Allows you to choose which programs any user on your computer can use; for instance, you might allow your spouse to run any program, but limit your children to only specific programs of your choosing

Monitoring Capabilities

Even more interesting is the monitoring and reporting capabilities of the parental controls in Vista. Figure 3.7 shows an example of the computer activity summary for a Windows user.

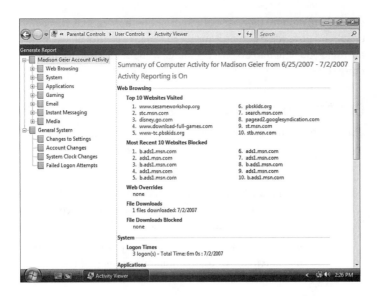

FIGURE 3.7

Example of a computer activity summary for a parental control–enabled user.

Here's a review of all the items contained in an activity report:

- Web browsing
  - Most commonly and most recently visited websites
  - Websites that were blocked because of restrictions imposed by Vista's parental controls
  - Web overrides permitting a restricted action and which administrator allowed it
  - Downloaded files (filename and location on your computer)
- System
  - Date, time, and duration of account sessions
- Applications
  - Recently used or blocked programs
  - Overrides permitting a restricted action and which administrator allowed it

- Gaming
  - Games played on your computer, including duration of gaming session and rating of the game
- Email
  - Received emails, including pertinent details of each message
  - Sent emails, including pertinent details of each message
  - Changes to contact lists along with the details
- Details of instant messaging
  - General instant messaging sessions
  - Web Cam and audio messaging sessions
  - Messaging in games
  - Files and links exchanged during instant messaging sessions
  - SMS messages sent to mobile phones
  - Changes to contact lists along with the details
- Media
  - Media (music, movies, and so on) that were played, including details such as song and album titles and their ratings
- General system
  - Setting changes with details such as which accounts apply to the change and which account performed the change
  - Changes to Windows account settings, including details such as what was changed and which account made the change
  - Changes to the system clock
  - Failed logon attempts

Accessing the Parental Controls

The parental controls can be accessed via the icon in Control Panel.

The Parental Controls screen, as shown in Figure 3.8, will appear listing the Windows accounts, along with a few global tasks on the left and a link to create additional users.

Clicking on an account will open another screen, as shown in Figure 3.9, to edit its individual parental control settings.

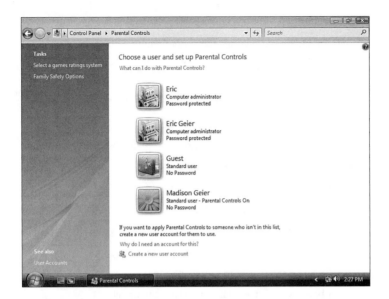

FIGURE 3.8

First screen after opening parental controls.

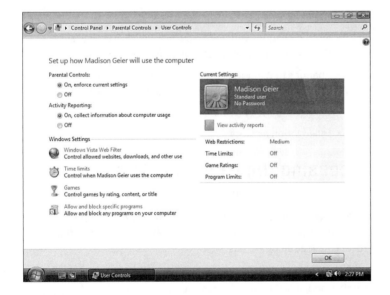

FIGURE 3.9

Screen showing a user's parental control settings.

To enable the parental controls for the chosen account, check the On, Enforce Current Settings option. Then specify if you want to record the activity and make other desired changes to the settings. You can access the settings by clicking the categories in the Windows Settings section. For quick access to certain settings, you can click on the status of the items, on the right side of the window, in the Current Settings section.

19 Windows Defender and Windows Firewall

Windows Vista includes Windows Firewall, just as Windows XP offered, which provides protection against hackers and Internet attacks by regulating inbound and outbound Internet access. Windows Vista, though, offers even more protection from Internet attackers and pests with anti-spyware and adware software called Windows Defender.

Accessing the Security Tools

Similar to Windows XP, Vista includes Windows Security Center, which provides quick status and configuration of security tools and programs. Windows Update and Internet Options are also displayed in the center with Windows Defender and Windows Firewall.

Here's how to access Windows Security Center:

1. Open the Start menu.
2. Click Control Panel.
3. Double-click the Security Center icon.

Figure 3.10 shows an example of the Windows Security Center.

You can also independently access Windows Defender and Windows Firewall via their icons in the Control Panel.

 TIP

You can also use Windows Defender on Windows XP computers running Service Pack 2.

To download, go to www.microsoft.com/downloads and search/browse for Windows Defender.

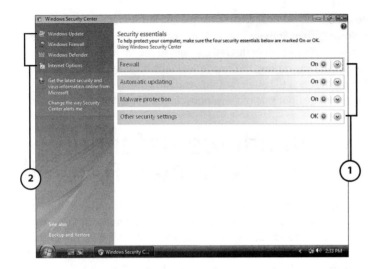

1 Status of security components

2 Links to access individual security components

FIGURE 3.10

Example of the first screen of Windows Security Center.

Touring Windows Defender

After Windows Defender is opened, you can quickly see the status of the program, such as the date of the last update and scan. Figure 3.11 shows an example.

1 Status information

2 Click here for a Quick scan or use arrow for Full System or Custom scans.

3 Click here to see details of past scans and alerts.

4 Click here to change Windows Defender options.

FIGURE 3.11

Example of Windows Defender.

Clicking the Scan button will perform a Quick scan, which checks for spyware and adware in the commonly infected areas of your computer. As pointed out in Figure 3.11, Full System and Custom scans can be executed by clicking the arrow next to the Scan button and selecting the desired option.

The History page, accessed via the History button (shown in Figure 3.11), displays the details of past actions, such as scans and alerts.

Clicking on the Tools button (shown in Figure 3.11) gives you access to settings and items such as automatic scanning and action preferences, scanning exclusions, and quarantined items.

Touring Windows Firewall

Windows Firewall also gives you a quick look at its status, as shown in Figure 3.12. Windows Firewall will report whether it's enabled and providing protection. You also can see a breakdown of your current firewall settings.

(1) Status information

(2) Click here to configure settings.

(3) Shortcuts to settings

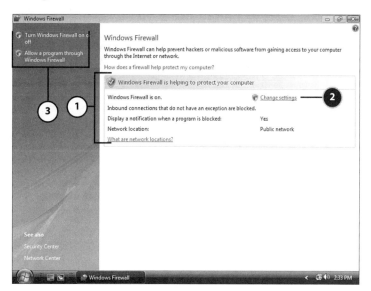

FIGURE 3.12

Example of Windows Firewall.

The Windows Firewall settings can be accessed by the Change Settings link, also shown in Figure 3.12. The Windows Firewall Settings window (Figure 3.13 shows an example) allows you to turn the protection on and off, exclude certain programs and services from the firewall, and choose which network connections to protect.

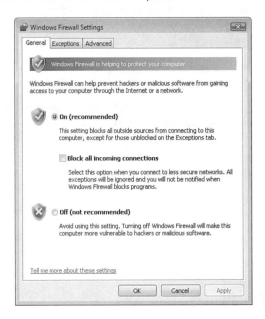

FIGURE 3.13

Change Windows Firewall settings here.

Figure 3.17 also points out the links that provide shortcuts to certain Windows Firewall settings.

20 Network and Sharing Center

One of the most obvious and needed changes Microsoft made with Vista is the increased networking security and improved intuitiveness of its networking settings. In Windows XP, the networking configuration features were spread between many different dialog boxes. Vista, how-ever, consolidates all of its network settings and features under one applet known as the Network and Sharing Center, which provides a one-stop shop for all your networking and Internet configuration needs.

Accessing the Network and Sharing Center

You can access the Network and Sharing Center via many methods:

- Right-click on the Network Status icon in the system tray, as shown in Figure 3.14.

1 Right-click on the Network Status icon in the system tray...

2 ...and select Network and Sharing Center.

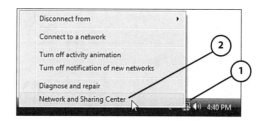

FIGURE 3.14

Accessing the Network and Sharing Center via the Network Status icon.

- Double-click on the Network Status icon in the system tray.
- Double-click on the Network and Sharing Center icon in Control Panel.
- Click on the Network and Sharing Center button on the toolbar when viewing your network, as shown in Figure 3.15.

1 Click here to open the Network and Sharing Center.

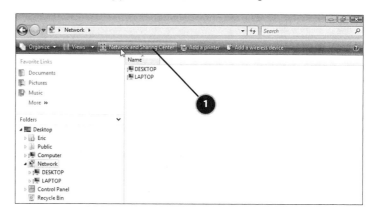

FIGURE 3.15

Accessing the Network and Sharing Center via the Network window.

Touring the Network and Sharing Center

As you can see in Figure 3.16, the Network and Sharing Center provides visual diagrams and maps of your home or office network. The full map that's accessible from this center provides an easy way to access any shared resources of other PCs and devices on the network.

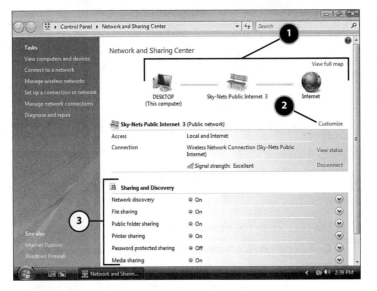

1. Depiction of the network

2. Click here to customize the network settings.

3. Sharing and discovery status

FIGURE 3.16

Example of the Network and Sharing Center.

Just below the network map in the Network and Sharing Center, you can view and access your connection information. The Customize link allows you to change the name of the network connection, the type (private or public), and the icon given to the network connection, such as the bench you see in Figure 3.16.

Next, you're provided with the status of all the main sharing and discovery settings and the ability to make quick changes, which is a big enhancement from XP.

Another exceptional improvement is the set of links (see Figure 3.17) at the bottom of the window, showing all the files and folders your account and computer are sharing on the network.

As a final point, the tasks pane on the left side of the window provides access to familiar connectivity settings and tasks, as well as a shortcut to the Internet Options and Wireless Firewall settings.

(1) Click these links to see what you're sharing.

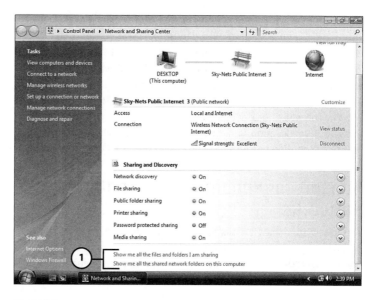

FIGURE 3.17

Links in Network and Sharing Center.

New Network Classification Scheme

In Windows Vista, the first time you connect to a network, you must classify its location/type: Home, Work, or Public (see Figure 3.18).

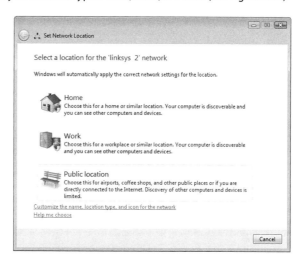

FIGURE 3.18

Example of pop-up window to classify network type.

This new scheme is extremely useful as it automatically modifies the appropriate network settings based upon the location type you choose. For example, suppose you connect to the Wi-Fi hot spot at your local café; you would choose Public location. Then, Vista will automatically disable all network discovery and sharing to protect your documents and privacy while on the unsecured network. Then, suppose you went back home and connected to your home network, naturally classified as a Home location. Windows Vista would then allow network discovery and sharing because you trust the other users on the network.

Support for Nonbroadcasting Wireless Networks

Windows Vista makes it easier to use wireless networks that do not broadcast their Service Set Identifier (SSID), also known as the network name. In Windows XP, these types of networks didn't appear on the list of available wireless networks; however, they now appear as unnamed networks in Windows Vista, as shown in Figure 3.19.

> **▶ NOTE**
>
> SSID is a sequence of 32 or fewer letters and/or numbers that identifies your wireless network.
>
> As a low-level security measure, some wireless network administrators (in homes and businesses) chose not to broadcast their SSID. This prevents the average PC user with Windows XP from even knowing that their network exists, and hides the SSID from Windows Vista users.

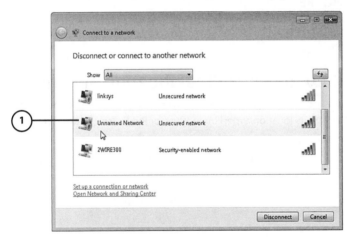

1 Unnamed wireless networks appear in Vista.

FIGURE 3.19

Example of hidden Wi-Fi networks on the Vista network list.

Instead of having to manually add a nonbroadcasting wireless network to the preferred network list to connect, all you have to do in Vista is select the Unnamed Network, click Connect, and enter the SSID when prompted (and enter the security key if encryption is enabled).

You might think that this degrades the security that hidden networks offer; however, the SSID is still needed to connect to the network. In addition, not broadcasting your SSID doesn't offer a whole lot of security anyway.

21 Instant Search and Internet Explorer 7

Windows Vista offers better searching methods than any other previous version of Windows. The Instant Search feature allows you to search through a prebuilt index or catalog of defined areas of your computer, such as documents, programs, email messages, web favorites, and history. This method allows for much quicker results. In fact, the new search features are so good, it's probable that you'll find what you are looking for before you're even done typing a keyword into the Search box.

You can use Instant Search via many locations and Windows applications, such as:

- Start menu
- Windows Explorer and Computer
- Windows Photo Gallery (see Figure 3.20)

(1) Type your search terms here and press Enter.

FIGURE 3.20

Instant Search box in Photo Gallery.

For more information on using Instant Search, see #81, "Search from the Start Menu."

Internet Explorer 7 also offers a new search method, called Live Search, for Internet searching. This feature makes it possible to search many different search engines from one field (see Figure 3.21). Not only can you add popular general search engines (Google, Yahoo!, and so on), you can add virtually any website that has search functionality. This offers a very convenient way to search through your favorite sites.

For more information on using Live Search, see #95, "Add Providers to Live Search in Internet Explorer 7."

22 Photo Gallery

Unlike earlier versions of Windows, Vista includes photo and video organization and editing software, called Windows Photo Gallery. This is particularly handy for families with digital cameras and camcorders. Although it might not include all the bells and whistles third-party software packages might offer, it can help you organize and show off those digital photos and videos you probably have scattered about your hard drive.

Figure 3.22 and the following bullets give you a look into the main functions of Windows Photo Gallery.

FIGURE 3.21

Example of using Live Search in Internet Explorer 7.

FIGURE 3.22

Example of Windows Photo Gallery.

(1) Click here to edit and enhance the selected photo.

(2) Click here to print selected photos.

- **Viewing and organizing:** You can effortlessly browse through your photos and videos in a Thumbnails view, navigating by assigned tags and ratings, date taken, folders, or simply all available media. Hovering over a photo or video will display a larger image for better viewing. In addition, double-clicking on them brings them into the dedicated viewer and is where you can assign the tags and ratings. You can also organize the photos into separate folders by right-clicking on the folders and creating subfolders.

- **Fix:** Selecting a photo and clicking the Fix button allows you to fine-tune the image by adjusting exposure and color, cropping, and removing red eye. In addition, an auto adjust feature can make automated enhancements.

- **Print:** Windows Photo Gallery doesn't just offer simple photo printing; it can automatically adjust for printing various sizes, including 4x6, 5x7, 8x10, and wallets. Simply choose a photo (or multiple photos), select the Print menu, and click Print to get started.

- **Make CD and DVD movies:** Windows Photo Gallery makes it easy to export photos and videos to Windows Movie and DVD makers. This allows you to create movies and presentations of images and clips, which make incredible keepsakes and gifts. You can either select particular media and choose Data-disc or Video DVD from the Burn menu, or click the Make a Movie button.

> **NOTE**
>
> The Windows DVD Maker and other DVD capabilities are only included with the Home Premium and Ultimate editions of Windows Vista. However, when using other editions, you can still use Windows Movie Maker, which you can use to create video CDs or export to your PC.

23 Windows Aero and Windows Flip

All editions of Windows Vista include a new look and functionality, as discussed earlier in #17, "New Look and Functionality." However, if you've chosen Home Premium or better and meet certain system requirements, the Windows Aero interface provides even more enhanced looks and features.

Figure 3.23 shows examples of some appearance enhancements of Windows Aero, such as the live thumbnails on the taskbar, task switch, and translucent title bars on opened windows.

Another feature gained when using Windows Aero is Windows Flip 3D, which offers a method to quickly switch among opened windows and applications. As you can see in Figure 3.24, it gives you live images of the windows you can flip through.

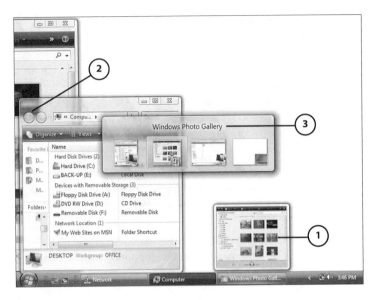

① Hover over applications for the live thumbnails.

② Translucent title bars

③ Press Alt+Tab for live thumbnails of opened applications.

FIGURE 3.23

Interface and appearance enhancements to this version of Windows.

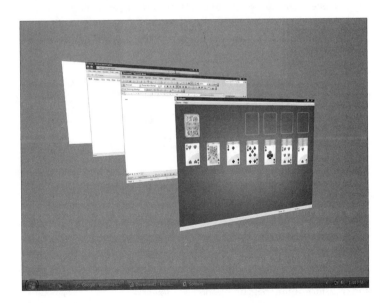

FIGURE 3.24

Example of Flip 3D.

The old method of switching among applications using Alt+Tab is also enhanced by Windows Aero. Instead of just showing the icon and titles of opened windows, it also gives you a live thumbnail image. See Figure 3.23 for an example.

For more information on using Windows Flip 3D, see #94, "Change Windows Using Flip 3D."

24 Windows Mobility Center and Tablet PC Support

Windows Mobility Center and Tablet PC support provides for a better mobile computing experience. Windows Mobility Center is a one-stop shop for settings and preferences related to mobile computing, available on laptops running on all Windows Vista editions except Home Basic.

This center provides access to power management settings, which can help you save battery life and customize your Power buttons. It also contains settings for multiple monitors so you can use an external display for a presentation or extend your desktop among multiple monitors. In addition, specific presentation and network projection features are included to give you a quicker and seamless presentation experience.

Windows HotStart is another feature gained from the Windows Mobility Center. This allows you to specify HotStart buttons on your mobile computer to open particular media files or applications. HotStart buttons can even be used when the computer is sleeping, hibernating, or off, enabling quick access to media and applications, while saving battery life.

Here's how to access the Windows Mobility Center:

1. Open the Start menu.
2. Click Control Panel.
3. Double-click the Windows Mobility Center icon.

Windows Vista provides better Tablet PC support with enhanced handwriting error detection and automatic learning. By using your mouse to write or using an onscreen keyboard, you can enter text without using a standard keyboard. As shown in Figures 3.25 and 3.26, these Tablet PC tools emulate the feel of real keyboarding with Tablet PCs.

FIGURE 3.25

Tablet PC keyboard.

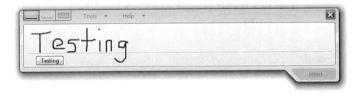

FIGURE 3.26

Tablet PC handwriting to text device.

You can access the Tablet PC tools on the Start menu:

1. Open the Start menu.

2. Click All Programs.

3. Click Accessories.

4. Click the Tablet PC directory.

25 Windows Meeting Space

Windows Meeting Space, available in all Vista editions except Home Basic, allows you to connect with others around you to share files, applications, or control of your entire computer. Although Windows Meeting Space doesn't support connections over the Internet, it is very useful for in-person meetings or a meeting with all participants in the same building.

For example, instead of several people in a meeting gathering around a PC or laptop trying to see the screen, Windows Meeting Space allows people to see the live image of the screen on their own computer, as shown in Figure 3.27. You can connect with each other over a wired or wireless network or by using a peer-to-peer (ad hoc) wireless connection.

1 Remote PC's desktop

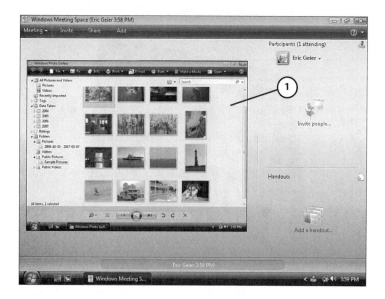

FIGURE 3.27

Example of viewing the desktop of a participant in a Windows Meeting Space session.

You can access Windows Meeting Space on the All Programs section of the Start menu.

26 Windows SideShow

Windows SideShow is a new technology developed by Microsoft to enable real-time viewing of information, data, and media from your computer, on secondary displays and mobile devices. For example, you could check your email, contacts, and appointments without turning on your main computer.

Windows SideShow is available in all Vista editions except Home Basic.

Compatible Devices

Devices and products compatible with this technology should have a Windows SideShow logo displayed on the box.

The following are a few examples of devices that could support
Windows SideShow:

  ■ Laptop lid displays, as shown in Figure 3.28

FIGURE 3.28

*Example of a laptop with external Windows SideShow-compatible display;
courtesy of ASUS Computer, Inc.*

  ■ Keyboards
  ■ Mobile phones
  ■ Digital picture frames, as shown in Figure 3.29

FIGURE 3.29

*Example of a Windows SideShow-compatible digital picture frame;
courtesy of I-Mate, PLC.*

Gadgets

Gadgets (or add-ons) give Windows SideShow devices their functionality. Windows Mail and Windows Media Player are two gadgets that are automatically included with Windows Vista. Using the Windows Mail gadget, for example, allows you to view your email messages from Windows Mail on your Windows SideShow device.

There are many more gadgets you can install for additional functionalities, such as the following:

- Picture viewers
- Weather applications (such as WeatherBug)
- Feed and RSS readers
- Support for email services (such as GMail)
- Stock market tickers

Keep in mind that the compatibility of gadgets is dependent upon the Windows SideShow device.

Installing and Setting Up Devices

For Windows SideShow devices separate from your computer, you must install/set up the device with your computer. You should follow the vendor or manufacturer directions. Then after the device installation, you can customize your device and configure the gadgets.

Here's how to access the Windows SideShow settings:

1. Open the Start menu.
2. Click Control Panel.
3. Double-click the Windows SideShow icon.

27 Windows Automatic Backup

For Windows Vista Home Basic and Home Premium users, Windows Automatic Backup (shown in Figure 3.30) is included to help protect your personal files and documents against accidental deletion and loss. You can set up Windows Automatic Backup to periodically copy your personal files and documents to another location, such as a secondary hard drive, flash drive, or network folder.

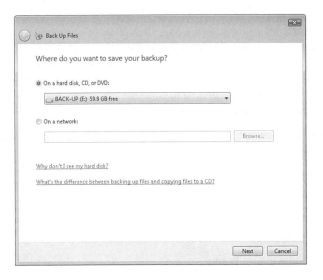

FIGURE 3.30

Windows Automatic Backup.

Your computer's system and program files, Windows settings, and applications are not included in the backup. This is because Windows Vista and your applications should be able to be reinstalled with your CDs and DVDs, whereas your personal files and documents might not be replaceable.

If you do experience system problems or discover you accidentally deleted or modified a file, you can also use the restore functionality of Windows Automatic Backup.

Here's how to access the Windows backup features:

1. Open the Start menu.
2. Click Control Panel.
3. Double-click the Backup and Restore Center icon.

 TIP

Keep in mind another feature called System Restore basically provides the backup and protection of your system files, which is skipped in Windows Automatic Backup.

You can quickly access this feature by entering "System Restore" into the Search box on the Start menu and pressing Enter.

28 Windows Complete PC Backup and Restore

For Windows Vista Business and Ultimate edition users, Windows Complete PC Backup and Restore (shown in Figure 3.31) is included to help protect your system against accidental deletion and loss. Unlike Windows Automatic Backup (for lower Vista editions), Windows Complete PC Backup and Restore provides total backup capabilities. The system files and your applications can also be preserved with your personal files and documents.

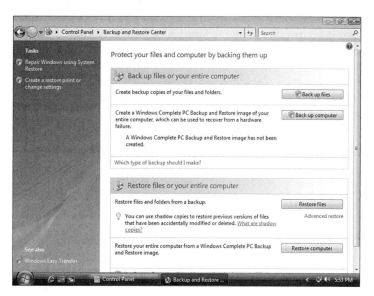

FIGURE 3.31

Windows Complete PC Backup and Restore.

In addition to restoring your entire system in an event of a serious system issue, you can also apply the backup to another PC. This is convenient if you need to send your PC in for repair or you would just like to change PCs.

Here's how to access the Windows backup features:

1. Open the Start menu.

2. Click Control Panel.

3. Double-click the Backup and Restore Center icon.

29 Windows Media Center

Windows Media Center is an innovative application, available in the Home Premium and Ultimate editions, that takes your media viewing and presentation to another level. Beyond the photo slideshows that make images come to life and the music explorer that displays the album art and information, Windows Media Center allows you to record TV and movies. If you don't have a TV tuner loaded in your PC to do the recording, you can still view previews and clips from many popular shows and cable networks.

You can even display the media from your computer to your TV, using a wireless or wired network and an additional piece of hardware called a Media Center Extender. You then can use Windows Media Center on your TV, just like you would in front of your PC. However, you can more practically display and present your pictures and videos, from the comfort of your living room.

 TIP

You can choose from many brands of Media Center Extenders. You can use networked digital media players, such as an Xbox 360 or other digital media receivers (DMR) from brands like D-Link and Linksys.

Accessing Windows Media Center

You can open Windows Media Center from the Start menu:

1. Open the Start menu.
2. Click All Programs.
3. Click Windows Media Center.

Touring Windows Media Center

Windows Media Center will open to the main menu (shown in Figure 3.32), where you can choose the desired media type. You can use the arrows that appear when hovering on the top and bottom of the list to scroll through the media types. Then, you can use the left and right arrows to scroll through the options for the particular media type.

You can use the left arrow, in the upper-left corner of the screen to return to the previous screen. In addition, you can return to the main menu by clicking the Windows Media Center icon.

FIGURE 3.32

Windows Media Center.

30 Windows DVD Maker

Windows Vista Home Premium and Ultimate editions come with the Windows DVD Maker. This application allows you to create DVDs of video and photo slideshows to view from your TV. You can even create custom menus and play your favorite tunes during the slideshows. These DVDs can make irreplaceable keepsakes and gifts for the family.

You can access the Windows DVD Maker on the Start menu:

1. Open the Start menu.
2. Click All Programs.
3. Click Windows DVD Maker, as shown in Figure 3.33.

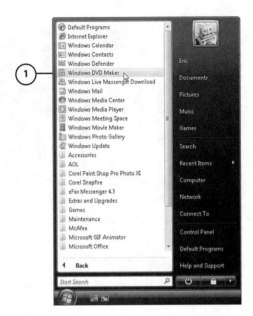

 Click here to open
Windows DVD Maker.

FIGURE 3.33

Opening Windows DVD Maker.

31 Games

Even the long-beloved Windows games (such as Solitaire and Minesweeper) have been redesigned and enhanced with better graphics and sound effects.

The following games are included with all Windows Vista editions:

- Freecell
- Hearts
- Minesweeper
- Purble Place
- Solitaire
- Spider Solitaire

All the games except Purble Place (see example in Figure 3.34) were in Windows XP. This is a nice addition to the Windows games as it's great for younger users, 6 years and up. The three different games challenge your memory and matching skills.

> **NOTE**
>
> The Internet games that were included with Windows XP have been removed from Windows Vista. You can, however, still access those games and more at http://zone.msn.com.

FIGURE 3.34

Purble Place game included with Windows Vista.

Four new premium games are also included with Windows Vista Ultimate and Home Premium editions:

- Chess Titans
- Mahjong Titans
- InkBall
- Windows Hold'em (Ultimate only)

You can access all the Windows games from the Start menu:

1. Open the Start menu.
2. Click All Programs.
3. Click the Games directory.

32 Windows Fax and Scan

Available in the Business and Ultimate editions, Windows Fax and Scan (shown in Figure 3.35) is an improved and enhanced version of the fax services Windows XP offered. You can now create cover sheets onscreen to be used with your fax or include files to be faxed. Of course, scanning capabilities have also been integrated. In addition, improvements have been made, such as support for scanning documents to include with faxes and support for network-connected scanners.

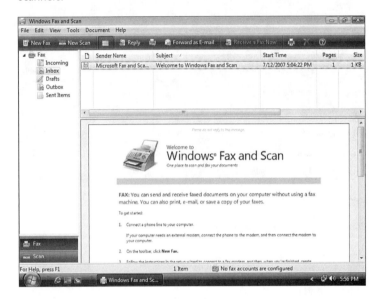

FIGURE 3.35

Windows Fax and Scan.

33 Remote Desktop Connection

Another feature only available to Windows Vista Business and Ultimate users is Remote Desktop Connection, shown in Figure 3.36. Just like in Windows XP Professional, Remote Desktop Connection allows you to connect to other PCs on your network or over the Internet.

Remote Desktop Connection takes network sharing to another level. Rather than just being able to view and use files from other computers, Remote Desktop Connection allows you to view a remote computer's desktop just as if you were sitting in front of the computer. Therefore, you could use applications in addition to files and documents.

FIGURE 3.36

Remote Desktop Connection.

For example, you could periodically work from a laptop in your home or office, but use applications and files from your desktop PC.

34 Shadow Copy

Another data-protection tool you can use among other traditional system backup and safeguard techniques is Shadow Copy. It is available and enabled by default in Windows Vista Business and Ultimate editions. Shadow Copy is particularly useful in helping recover previous versions of files. For example, when you accidentally save over a file or notice you've made changes to files that you now regret, you can easily revert to other saved versions. A few clicks and the file will appear just as it did back when it was saved days or months ago.

Shadow Copy works in conjunction with System Protection, and its System Restore features. Therefore, System Protection must be enabled for Shadow Copy to work. Shadow copies of files are made when restore points are saved, typically every day.

 TIP

The System Protection features are hard-drive independent; therefore, you would need to turn on System Protection for each hard drive and/or partition.

To access the System Protection settings, right-click the Computer icon on the Start menu or desktop, select Properties, and click the System Protection link under the Tasks pane on the left.

Here's how to access the Shadow Copy feature:

1. Right-click on the file or folder to restore.

2. Select Restore Previous Versions, as shown in Figure 3.37.

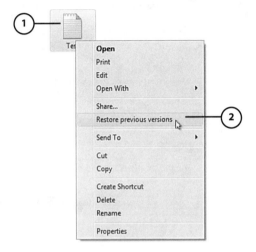

① Right-click on a file or folder.

② Select Restore Previous Versions.

FIGURE 3.37

Using the Shadow Copy feature for a particular file or folder.

35 Windows BitLocker Drive Encryption

Windows BitLocker Drive Encryption, only available in Windows Vista Ultimate, helps secure your data and documents in case your computer is lost or stolen. By encrypting the entire Windows volume, BitLocker Drive Encryption ensures no one can break into Windows and retrieve user information and documents.

This feature is incredibly valuable if you store sensitive data on your computer, such as business and customer data or personal banking information, especially on laptops, which can be easily stolen or misplaced.

Here's how to access the Windows BitLocker Drive Encryption settings:

1. Open the Start menu.

2. Click Control Panel.

3. Double-click the BitLocker Drive Encryption icon.

36 Language Packs

The language packs offered by Microsoft for Windows Vista Ultimate allow you to set the entire interface of Windows to another language. It is even user account specific, so you can set different languages for the individual users on the same PC.

The language packs can be downloaded from the Windows Ultimate Extras section on the Windows Update website:

www.update.microsoft.com

Here's how to access the language settings (such as to remove a language pack):

1. Open the Start menu.
2. Click Control Panel.
3. Double-click the Regional and Language Options icon.
4. Click the Keyboards and Languages tab.
5. Refer to the Display language section, as shown in Figure 3.38.

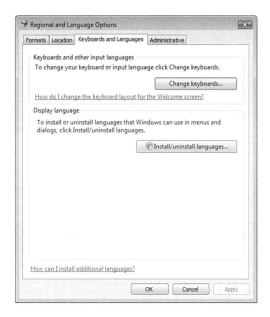

FIGURE 3.38

Display language section.

4

Changing the Look and Feel of Vista

Windows Vista's new neat-and-slick interface might make you ooh and aah, might wow you, and might even be the reason you updated to Vista; on the other hand, you might not care for it and might not want to take the time to get used to it. Therefore, this chapter is dedicated to those who don't like change—especially when it comes to their PC. Additionally if your PC isn't one of the top-of-the-line machines you might experience better performance by tuning back the Vista interface enhancements.

This chapter contains step-by-step tasks and tips to convert Vista's new (and occasionally annoying) desktop and interface to one you'll easily recognize.

37 Banish the Welcome Center

By default, Windows Vista loads the Welcome Center each time Windows boots up. The Welcome Center does offer convenient links to things new Vista users might be interested in; however, after you think it's overextended its welcome, you can easily disable it.

Although disabling the Welcome Center is quite simple, it's easy to overlook things. All you have to do is check the Run at Startup option in the lower-left corner of the Welcome Center, as Figure 4.1 points out.

 Check this box to banish the Welcome Center.

FIGURE 4.1

Disabling the Welcome Center.

> **TIP**
>
> If you want to use the Welcome Center again, you can access it from the Control Panel: Simply click the Start menu, then choose Control Panel and select Welcome Center.

Now the Welcome Center won't bug you anymore when Windows starts up!

38 Disable Windows Sidebar

Just like the Welcome Center, the new Windows Sidebar feature is set to automatically load each time you enter Windows Vista. This can be

TIP

Before totally blowing off this new feature, you might want to look into it more. Windows Sidebar and the gadgets can be very convenient and time saving.

For more information, you can check out #75, "Add More Gadgets to Sidebar."

annoying if you aren't making use of the sidebar's gadgets. If that's your case, you can easily disable Windows Sidebar from popping up.

Here's how to disable Windows Sidebar:

1. Right-click on Sidebar Windows and select Properties, as shown in Figure 4.2.

(1) Right-click on Windows Sidebar.

(2) Select Properties from the shortcut menu.

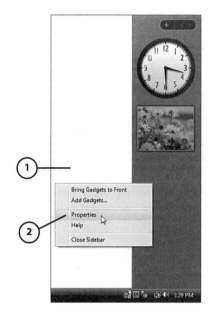

FIGURE 4.2

Accessing Windows Sidebar properties.

 TIP

If you want to simply close Windows Sidebar without disabling it from coming up at startup, just right-click on the Sidebar and click Close Sidebar.

2. Uncheck the Start Sidebar when Windows Starts option, as shown in Figure 4.3.

3. Click OK.

FIGURE 4.3

Disabling the Windows Sidebar from loading at startup.

① Click this check box to
rid yourself of the
Sidebar.

39 Change Windows Themes

Windows uses themes to make altering your desktop and interface easier. A theme contains a saved configuration for the appearance of your desktop background, icons, window styles, screensavers, and other personalization settings. Windows Vista comes preloaded with two themes: Windows Vista (enabled by default, of course) and Windows Classic, which resembles the appearance of Windows 98 and Millennium Edition (Me).

The first task in getting rid of the Vista look and feel is applying the Windows Classic theme:

1. Right-click on your desktop and select Personalize, as shown in Figure 4.4.

2. Click on Theme, as shown in Figure 4.5.

FIGURE 4.4

Opening the personalization settings.

① Choose Themes from the Personalization window.

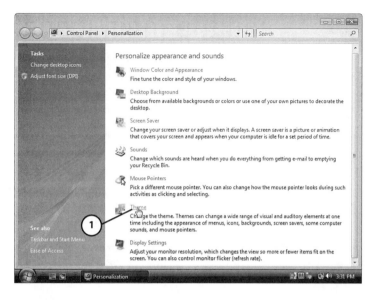

FIGURE 4.5

Accessing the theme settings.

3. Select Windows Classic from the drop-down list, as shown in Figure 4.6, and then click OK to exit.

① Choose Windows Classic to go back to a more familiar Windows interface.

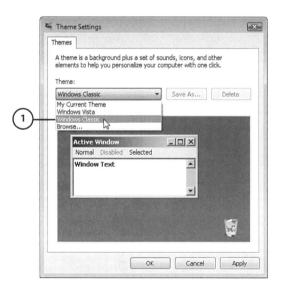

FIGURE 4.6

Selecting the Windows Classic theme.

40 Add the Main Icons

As you probably noticed, the only icon that's placed on the desktop by default in Windows Vista is the Recycle Bin. However, if you're used to the others (such as My Computer or My Network Places) being on the desktop, you can easily add the other main icons:

1. Right-click on your desktop and select Personalize, as shown in Figure 4.7.

2. Click Change Desktop Icons in the tasks pane on the left, as shown in Figure 4.8.

3. Check the icons you want to appear on the desktop, such as that shown in Figure 4.9, and then click OK to exit.

FIGURE 4.7

Opening the personalization settings.

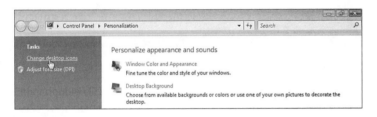

FIGURE 4.8

Accessing the desktop icon settings.

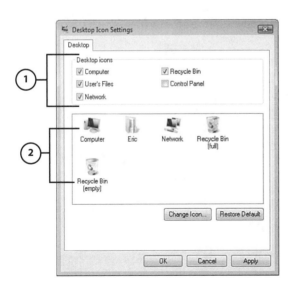

(1) Check these boxes...

(2) ...to select which of these icons you want to appear on your desktop.

FIGURE 4.9

Example of selecting additional icons to appear on the desktop.

41 Add the Microsoft Internet Explorer Icon

Along with the other main icons, the icon for Internet Explorer isn't automatically placed on the Vista desktop. In addition, the Internet Explorer icon can't even be enabled via the desktop icon settings, such as discussed in the previous section when adding the main icons. This can be rather bothersome when you're accustomed to clicking on the icon to surf the web. Nevertheless, there are ways to get the icon on your desktop.

Here's the simplest way to add the Internet Explorer icon to the desktop:

1. Open the Start menu.
2. Click and drag the Internet Explorer icon to the desktop, such as Figure 4.10 demonstrates.

① Click, hold, and drag the Internet Explorer icon.

② Drop the Internet Explorer icon on your desktop to create a shortcut.

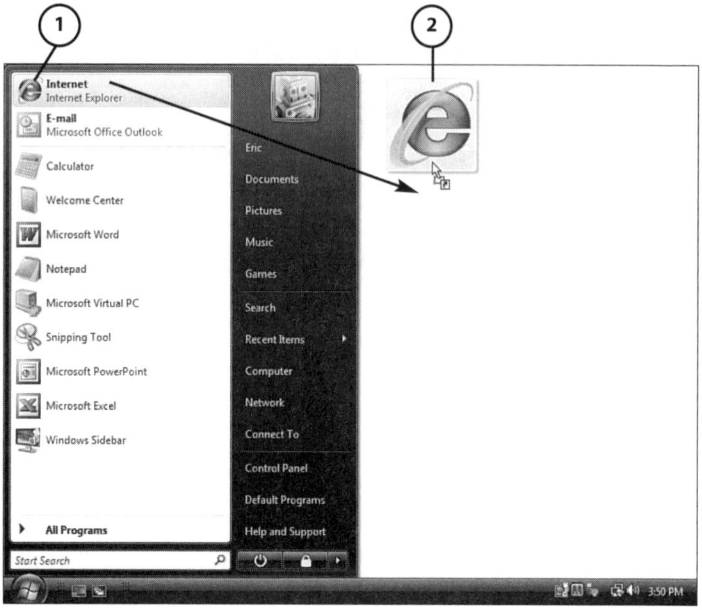

FIGURE 4.10

Dragging the Internet Explorer icon to the desktop to create a shortcut.

3. To get rid of the shortcut text, right-click on the icon, select Rename, and delete the word "Shortcut."

As seen in Figure 4.10, creating a simple shortcut means you'll have the ugly arrow on the Internet Explorer icon, unlike the other main icons, such as Computer, Network, and Recycle Bin.

There is a more advanced method of adding the Internet Explorer icon without the arrow; however, it requires editing the Windows Registry:

1. Open the Start menu.

2. If you are using the Vista Start menu, type "regedit" in the Search box and press Enter, as shown in Figure 4.11.

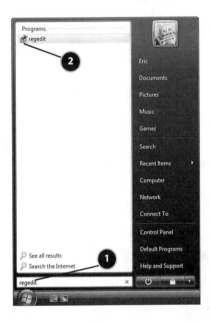

1. Type "regedit" in the Search box, and then press Enter.

2. The regedit program will appear here; double-click to run it.

FIGURE 4.11

Accessing the Registry Editor.

3. Navigate to the following folder, as demonstrated in Figure 4.12:

    HKEY_CURRENT_USER\Software\Microsoft\Windows\
    CurrentVersion\Explorer\HideDesktopIcons\NewStartPanel

 CAUTION

Be very careful when editing the Windows Registry. Mistakes can cause major problems. By major, I mean everything from a program failing to start to your computer being made unusable. One false move in the Registry can spell disaster, so be careful!

It's also a good idea to make a backup copy prior to making any changes to the Registry. Here's how:

1. Open the Registry Editor by following steps 1 and 2.

2. In the Registry Editor, click File on the menu and select Export.

3. On the bottom of the dialog box, select the All option for the Export Range.

4. Browse, find, and select a location to save the registry. It's best to save it to a removable shortage device like a flash drive, floppy disc, or CD.

5. Enter your desired file name, such as Registry_Backup_*DATE*.

6. Click Save and wait until it's done which may take a few minutes.

 NOTE

If you are using the Windows Classic View, click Run on the Start Menu, type "regedit", click OK, and proceed to step 3.

1 Carefully navigate here; click each parent folder to open its subfolders, just as you would when using Windows Explorer.

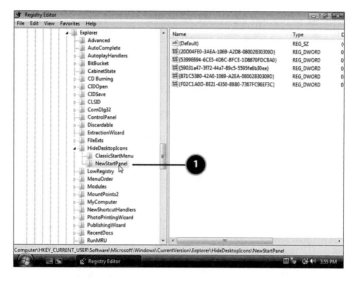

FIGURE 4.12

Navigating to the NewStartPanel registry folder.

4. In the right pane, double-click the following key, as shown in Figure 4.13:

{871C5380-42A0-1069-A2EA-08002B30309D}

1 Double-click this registry key.

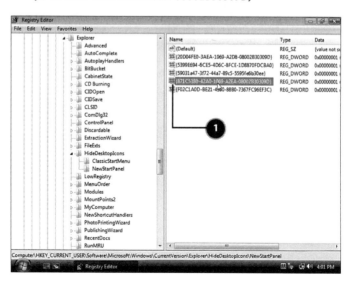

FIGURE 4.13

Opening the registry key properties.

WHAT IF THE REGISTRY KEY ISN'T THERE?

If the {871C5380-42A0-1069-A2EA-08002B30309D} key doesn't exist, you will need to create it. To add the key:

1. Right-click in the right pane, point to New, and click on DWORD (32-bit) Value, as shown in Figure 4.14.

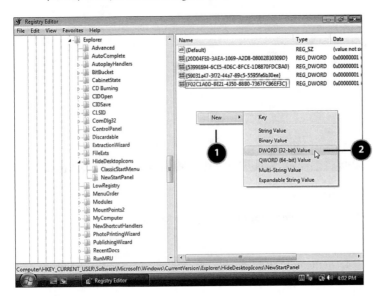

① Right-click on the right pane of the Registry.

② Choose this value.

FIGURE 4.14

Creating a new registry key entry.

2. Type {871C5380-42A0-1069-A2EA-08002B30309D} (including the curly braces) into the entry and press Enter. Figure 4.15 shows an example.

3. Then double-click on the new key and proceed to step 4.

1 Type the new registry key here, including the braces.

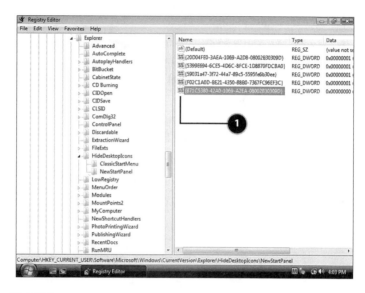

FIGURE 4.15

Entering the new registry key.

4. In the Value Data field, type "0," as shown in Figure 4.16, and then click OK.

1 Double-click on the new key you created.

2 Enter "0" in the Value Data field.

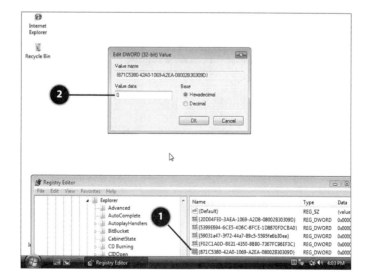

FIGURE 4.16

Inputting the new registry key value.

5. Close the Registry Editor.

6. To activate the Internet Explorer icon, right-click anywhere on the desktop and select Refresh, as shown in Figure 4.17.

7. The Internet Explorer icon should now appear on your desktop, as shown in Figure 4.18.

Add an Internet Explorer Icon in Windows Classic View

To add an Internet Explorer icon from within Windows Classic View:

1. Click on Run, as shown in Figure 4.19.

FIGURE 4.19

Opening the Run prompt.

2. Type "regedit", as shown in Figure 4.20, and click OK.

FIGURE 4.20

Accessing the Registry Editor.

FIGURE 4.17

Refreshing the desktop to activate the new Internet Explorer icon.

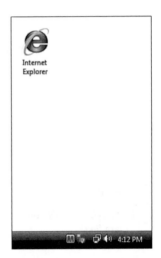

FIGURE 4.18

The new Internet Explorer icon.

① Type "regedit" into the Run dialog box.

3. Navigate to the following folder, as demonstrated in Figure 4.21:

HKEY_CURRENT_USER\Software\Microsoft\Windows\
CurrentVersion\Explorer\HideDesktopIcons\
ClassicStartMenu

① Find this registry folder and click it.

② The values in the ClassicStartMenu folder appear here.

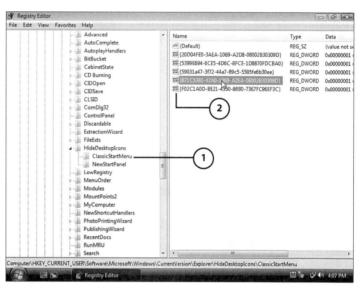

FIGURE 4.21

Navigating to the ClassicStartMenu registry folder.

NOTE

If the {871C5380-42A0-1069-A2EA-08002B30309D} key doesn't exist, you will need to create it, as explained earlier in this chapter in the sidebar titled "What if the Registry Key Isn't There?" However, create the registry key in the correct ClassicsStart Menufolder.

4. In the right pane, double-click the following key, as shown in Figure 4.22:

{871C5380-42A0-1069-A2EA-08002B30309D}

5. In the Value Data field, type "0", as shown in Figure 4.23, and then click OK.

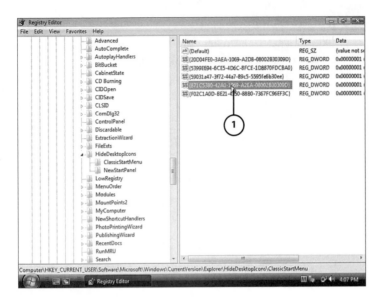

① Double-click this key.

FIGURE 4.22

Opening the registry key properties.

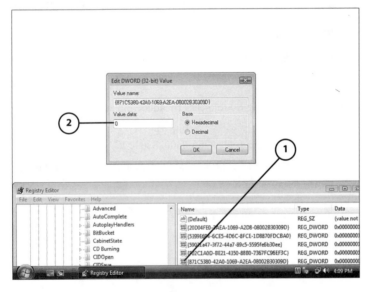

① Double-click on the new key you created.

② Enter "0" in the Value Data field.

FIGURE 4.23

Inputting the new registry key value.

42 Reduce Large Icons

As you might have noticed, Windows Vista's default icon size is a bit larger than in previous versions. Just in case you're the curious type, Figure 4.24 shows a side-by-side comparison of the default icon sizes for Windows XP (on the left) and Vista (on the right).

1 Windows XP icons

2 Windows Vista icons

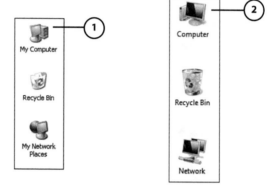

FIGURE 4.24

Comparison of icon sizes for Windows XP (on the left) and Vista (on the right).

These larger icons can be somewhat annoying and unnecessarily large. Fortunately, changing the icon size is incredibly painless; here's how to do it:

1. Right-click on the desktop.

2. Click on View and select Classic Icons, as shown in Figure 4.25.

 TIP

If the classic icon setting isn't small enough (or the Large Icons setting is not big enough) or if you just want to have some fun and play a prank on someone, see #80, "Resize Icons with the Mouse."

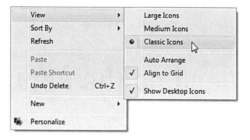

FIGURE 4.25

Changing to the classic icon size.

43 Rename the Computer Icon

Instead of My Computer, Windows Vista dropped the *My* and has renamed the icon to *Computer*. If you're particular about the naming of your icons or you find it hard to get used to the Computer icon after years of seeing My Computer, you can simply change it.

Here's how to rename the Computer icon:

1. Right-click on the Computer icon and select Rename, as shown in Figure 4.26.

TIP

By default, the Computer icon isn't displayed on the desktop. If you want to add this icon to the desktop, see #40, "Add the Main Icons."

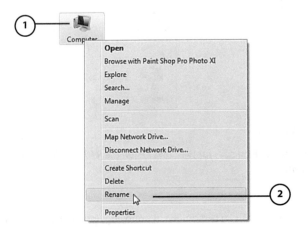

1. Right-click on the Computer icon.

2. Choose Rename.

FIGURE 4.26

Accessing the icon name.

FIGURE 4.27

Example of changing the Computer icon back to My Computer.

2. Enter your desired name, such as that shown in Figure 4.27.

3. Press Enter to save the new icon name.

44 Rename the Network Icon

The My Network Places icon has been renamed to simply *Network* in Windows Vista. If you're particular about the naming of your icons or you find it hard to get used to the Network icon after years of seeing My Network Places, you can change it. You can't simply click on the icon

TIP

By default, the Network icon isn't displayed on the desktop. If you want to add this icon to the desktop, see #40, "Add the Main Icons."

CAUTION

Be very careful when editing the Windows Registry. Mistakes can cause major problems. By major, I mean everything from a program failing to start to your computer being made unusable. One false move in the Registry can spell disaster, so be careful!

It's also a good idea to make a backup copy prior to making any changes to the Registry. Here's how:

1. Open the Registry Editor by following steps 1 and 2.

2. In the Registry Editor, click File on the menu and select Export.

3. On the bottom of the dialog box, select the All option for the Export Range.

4. Browse, find, and select a location to save the registry. It's best to save it to a removable short-age device like a flash drive, floppy disc, or CD.

5. Enter your desired file name, such as Registry_Backup_*DATE*.

6. Click Save and wait until it's done which may take a few minutes.

and rename it like other icons. You'll have to do it through a more advanced method by editing the Windows Registry; here's how to do it:

1. Open the Start menu.

2. In the Search box, type "regedit", as shown in Figure 4.28, and then press Enter. If you are using the Windows Classic Start menu, you need to click Run, type "regedit", and then click OK.

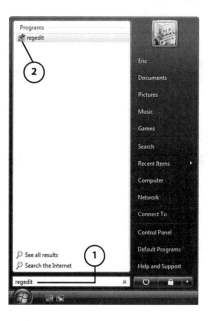

① Type "regedit" in the Search box, and then press Enter.

② The regedit program will appear here; double-click to run it.

FIGURE 4.28

Accessing the Registry Editor.

3. Navigate to the following folder, as demonstrated in Figure 4.29:

   HKEY_CURRENT_USER\Software\Classes\Local Settings\Software\Microsoft\Windows\Shell\MuiCache

4. Locate and double-click on the following Registry entry, as shown in Figure 4.30:

   @C:\Windows\system32\NetworkExplorer.dll,-1

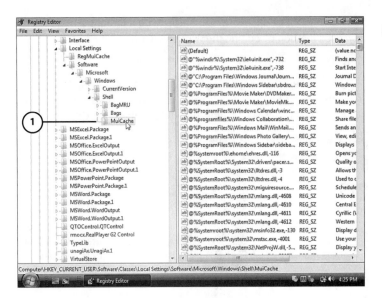

Navigate to this folder.

FIGURE 4.29

Navigating to the MuiCache registry folder.

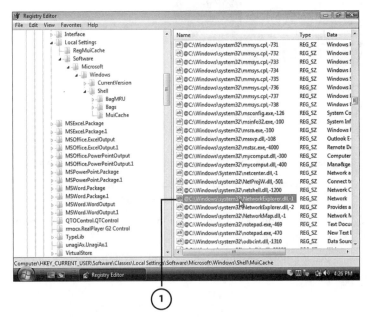

Double-click this entry.

FIGURE 4.30

Opening the registry key properties.

5. Enter your desired name in the Value Data field, as shown in Figure 4.31, and click OK.

1 Enter the desired name here.

FIGURE 4.31

Renaming the Network icon.

FIGURE 4.32

Refreshing the desktop to activate the new icon name.

6. Close the Registry Editor.

7. To activate the new icon name, right-click anywhere on the desktop and select Refresh. Figure 4.32 shows an example.

The new icon name should now appear, as shown in Figure 4.33.

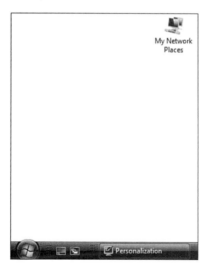

FIGURE 4.33

The new icon name.

45 Change to the Classic Start Menu

Even though you might have applied the Windows Classic theme from #39, "Change Windows Themes," the Start menu will have the new Vista functionality. For example, instead of the menus and folders expanding out when opened or hovered over, Vista's Start menu is a fixed size and provides a folder type style with scrollbars when navigating through programs.

If you find it's hard to adapt to this new design, you can apply the Classic Start menu:

1. Right-click on the taskbar and select Properties, as shown in Figure 4.34.

FIGURE 4.34

Accessing the taskbar properties.

2. Click the Start Menu tab.
3. Select the Classic Start menu option, as shown in Figure 4.35, and then click OK to exit.

 TIP

If you want to use the new search capabilities of the Start menu, you might not want to change to the Classic Start menu, as you'll get rid of this new feature.

For more information about this feature, see #17, "New Look and Functionality."

FIGURE 4.35

Selecting the Classic Start menu option.

46 Display the Log Off Button on the Start Menu

If you're a fan of the Log Off button that was on the Start menu of previous Windows versions, you might notice that it has disappeared, or, rather, it has moved to the menu accessed by the arrow, as shown in Figure 4.36.

This new location can be particularly frustrating if you have many user accounts on your PC and switch frequently. Nevertheless, you can bring the button back by personalizing the Classic Start menu:

1. Right-click on the taskbar and select Properties, as shown in Figure 4.37.

2. Click the Start Menu tab.

FIGURE 4.36

New Start menu location of the Log Off button.

FIGURE 4.37

Opening the taskbar properties.

3. Click the Customize button next to the Classic Start menu option, as shown in Figure 4.38.

4. Check the Display Log Off option, as shown in Figure 4.39, and then click OK to exit.

FIGURE 4.38

Accessing the customization settings for the Classic Start menu.

FIGURE 4.39

Enabling the Log Off for the Start menu.

TIP

Another modification you might be interested in is changing the Power button, located on the Start menu, to shut down your PC rather than put it to sleep. For more information, refer to #76, "Change Power Button on Start Menu."

47 Show Thumbnails of Pictures

By default in Windows XP, thumbnails for pictures are enabled when browsing the contents of your computer using My Computer or Windows Explorer. As you might know, the Thumbnails feature can come in handy when browsing through your digital photos and other images. Without the Thumbnails view, you have to open each image individually or use some type of photo software that provides thumbnail browsing.

The Thumbnails feature on Windows Vista is disabled by default. Nevertheless, you can easily enable this feature:

1. Double-click on the Computer (or My Computer) icon on your desktop.

   If the Computer icon isn't on the desktop, open Windows Explorer by opening the Start Menu, clicking All Programs, choosing Accessories, and clicking Windows Explorer.

2. Click on the Organize button on your toolbar, and select Folder and Search Options, as shown in Figure 4.40.

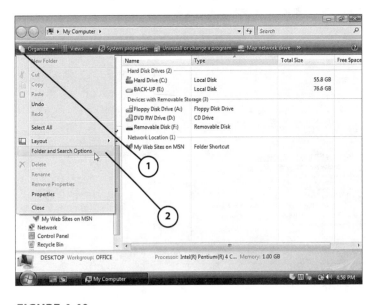

FIGURE 4.40

Accessing the folder options.

 TIP

Enabling thumbnails might affect your PC performance, making browsing through your files and folders a bit slower, which is worse on PCs loaded with lower memory. Therefore, if you don't need to browse through your pictures often or use photo software to view them, think about keeping the Thumbnails feature disabled.

 TIP

By default, the Computer icon isn't displayed on the desktop. If you want to add this icon to the desktop, see #40, "Add the Main Icons."

(**1**) Click here…

(**2**) …then select Folder and Search Options.

 TIP

If your toolbar isn't visible, press one of the Alt buttons on your keyboard to make it appear.

3. Click on the View tab.

4. Uncheck the Always Show Icons, Never Thumbnails option, as shown in Figure 4.41, and then click OK to exit.

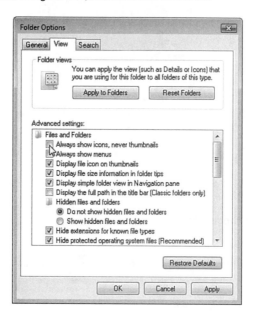

FIGURE 4.41

Enabling thumbnails of pictures.

 TIP

One thing you might find annoying about the tabs is that when you open a new one, it goes to a blank page. However, you can make new tabs go to your defined home page instead.

In addition, you can also define multiple home pages, so they load in separate tabs when opening Internet Explorer.

You might want to think about these two modifications before just getting rid of the tabs. You can see #96, "Change the Home Page of New Tabs in Internet Explorer 7," for more information.

48 Remove Tabbed Browsing from Internet Explorer 7

The new tabbing aspect in Internet Explorer can be useful; however, like other things with Windows Vista, you might not want to get used to the changes. You can get rid of this feature if you choose.

Here's how to disable the tabs:

1. Click on Tools and select Internet Options, as shown in Figure 4.42.

2. Click the Settings button in the Tabs section, as demonstrated in Figure 4.43.

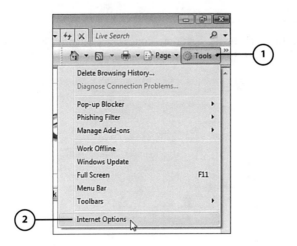

① Click here...

② ...and then choose Internet Options.

FIGURE 4.42

Opening the Internet Options.

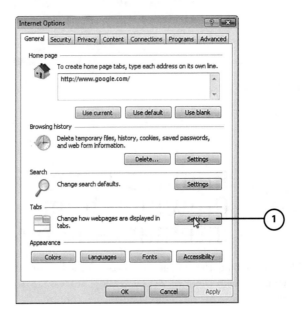

① Choose the Settings button in the Tabs options.

FIGURE 4.43

Accessing the tabs settings for Internet Explorer 7.

3. Uncheck the Enable Tabbed Browsing option, as shown in Figure 4.44, and then click OK to exit.

(1) Uncheck this setting.

FIGURE 4.44

Disabling the tabs feature for Internet Explorer 7.

4. You must close Internet Explorer and reopen it to use the new settings.

49 Display the Menu Bar in Internet Explorer 7

Just like most application windows in Vista, Internet Explorer 7 doesn't display the menu bar (for example the File, Edit, and Help menus) by default. This can be bothersome to those who are used to accessing the menu bar instead of using toolbar icons, and even then you have to become familiar with new icons. However, you can make the familiar menu bar reappear by using one of these two methods:

- Right-click on the Toolbar area, and select Menu Bar, as shown in Figure 4.45.

- Press one of the Alt buttons on your keyboard and the menu bar will appear, as shown in Figure 4.46.

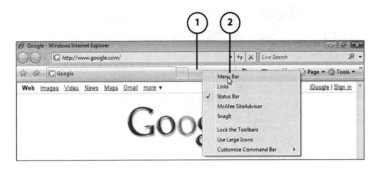

FIGURE 4.45

Displaying Internet Explorer's menu bar.

 Right-click on the Toolbar area.

 Select Menu Bar.

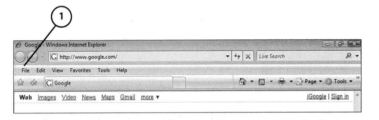

FIGURE 4.46

Displaying Internet Explorer's menu bar by using the Alt key.

(1) Like magic, the menu bar appears.

> **TIP**
>
> You can also use the Alt key in most other Windows applications/windows to make the menu bar appear.

5

Finding Your Way Around in Vista

After you begin using Vista, you'll definitely notice that some items aren't located exactly where they were in Windows XP. To make matters more confusing, some items have been renamed or changed. This can be frustrating; however, this chapter lists many of these relocated settings, preferences, and features. Use this chapter to help you get on your feet and be productive with Vista in no time.

5O Renamed Windows Applications

Among all the new features and changes in Vista, several applications have been renamed, as Table 5.1 shows.

Table 5.1 Renamed Applications

Old Name	New Name in Vista	Application Information
Windows Picture and Fax Viewer	Windows Photo Gallery (see Figure 5.1)	In addition to offering a way to view photos, Windows Photo Gallery helps you organize your digital photos and videos. It also allows you to fine tune the images and provides exceptional printing and movie and presentation making capabilities.
Outlook Express	Windows Mail (see Figure 5.2)	Windows Mail is an email client program for use with POP3 and IMAP accounts. Being a redesigned and improved version of Outlook Express, Windows Mail includes better features to combat issues such as junk email and phishing scams which try to fraudulently acquire your personal and sensitive information.
		Two other improved applications that interface with Windows Mail, in addition to being great standalone applications, are Windows Calendar and Windows Contacts.
Windows Address Book	Windows Contacts (see Figure 5.3)	Windows Contacts helps you keep track of contact and personal information of your family, friends, and colleagues.
		Similar to Windows Address Book, Windows Contacts is integrated with Windows Mail. It, however, has also been redesigned to provide better functionality for standalone use and its interface and features greatly improved.
Fax Console	Windows Fax and Scan (see Figure 5.4)	Like the other applications, Windows Fax and Scan is more user-friendly and includes enhancements. You can now create cover sheets onscreen to be used with your fax or include files to be faxed.
		Of course, scanning capabilities have also been integrated. In addition, improvements have been made, such as support for scanning documents to include with faxes and supporting network connected scanners.
NetMeeting	Windows Meeting Space (see Figure 5.5)	Even though Windows Meeting Space doesn't provide communication via the Internet as with NetMeeting, it is very useful for in-person meetings or a meeting with all participates in the same building. You can connect with each other over a wired or wireless network or by using a peer-to-peer (Ad hoc) wireless connection.

FIGURE 5.1

Windows Picture and Fax Viewer is now Windows Photo Gallery.

FIGURE 5.2

Outlook Express is now Windows Mail.

FIGURE 5.3

Windows Address Book is now Windows Contacts.

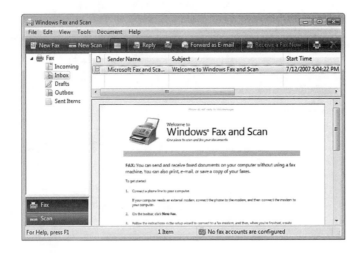

FIGURE 5.4

Fax Console is now Windows Fax and Scan.

> ➥ **NOTE**
>
> Windows Fax and Scan is included only in Windows Vista Business, Windows Vista Enterprise, and Windows Vista Ultimate.

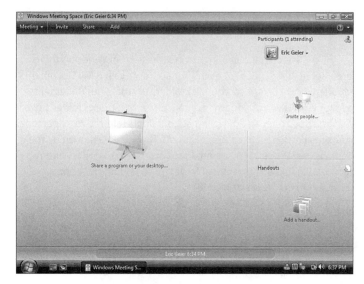

TIP

For more information about the new Windows Meeting Space, see #25, "Windows Meeting Space."

For more information about the new Windows Photo Gallery, see #22, "Photo Gallery."

FIGURE 5.5

NetMeeting is now Windows Meeting Space.

You can access all the applications mentioned in Table 5.1 from the Start menu, as pointed out in Figure 5.6.

① Open the Start menu, All Programs.

② Choose the program from the list.

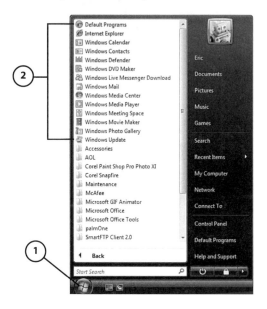

FIGURE 5.6

How to access the mentioned applications.

51 My Documents

As you might recall, in previous versions of Windows there were a set of folders (one for each user account), called My Documents that offered convenient categorized folders to store your documents and files. Windows Vista doesn't contain a My Documents folder; however, Vista does offer an equivalent set of folders referred to as personal folders (again, one for each user account). The folder is named by the Windows user account. For example, suppose you created a Windows account called Kids. The personal folder for that Windows account would automatically be labeled Kids.

Similar to Windows XP, you can access the personal folder from the Start menu, as shown in Figure 5.7 and in Windows Explorer, as shown in Figure 5.8.

① Open the Start menu.

② Personal folder for the currently logged-in user

FIGURE 5.7

Accessing the personal folder from the Start menu.

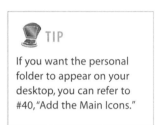

(1) Double-click the My Computer icon to open this window.

(2) Open the personal folder here.

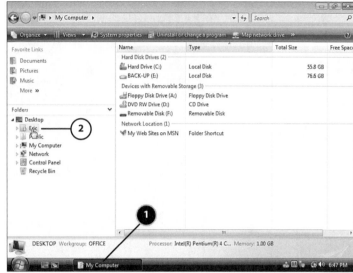

TIP

If you want the personal folder to appear on your desktop, you can refer to #40, "Add the Main Icons."

FIGURE 5.8

Accessing the personal folder in Windows Explorer.

After you open your personal folder, you'll notice that there have been quite a few additions to the three simple folders (My Pictures, My Videos, and My Music) Windows XP offered. As you can see in Figure 5.9, you now also have the following new folders and shortcuts to better help organize and access your documents and information:

- Contacts
- Desktop
- Documents
- Downloads
- Favorites
- Links
- Saved Games
- Searches

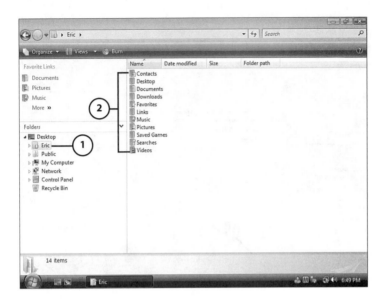

① Click here to see the contents of your personal folder.

② Personal folder contents are shown here.

FIGURE 5.9

The personal folder.

52 Shared Documents Folder

Instead of the Shared Documents folder, Windows Vista offers the Public folder. As Figure 5.10 shows, you can access the Public folder from Windows Explorer.

If you use the Public folder, you should keep in mind one important change from XP. Not only are the files contained in the Public folder open to other user accounts on the same computer, but now by default, access is open to other computers on any networks you might connect to, such as by other family members at home connected to the same router or by strangers when browsing the web at your local café.

Windows Vista does, however, have a security measure in place, which prompts you to classify the trustworthiness of the networks you connect to. This helps prevent unauthorized access of your documents when on public and other untrusted networks. See #20, "Network and Sharing Center," for more information.

 TIP

You can easily change the sharing status of the Public folder. Just open the Network and Sharing Center (by right-clicking on the Network Status icon in the system tray); the status and ability to change the setting is in the Sharing and Discovery section.

FIGURE 5.10

Accessing the Public folder in Windows Explorer.

53 View the Folder Path

As you might notice, unlike Windows XP, Vista doesn't show the "raw" folder path (for example, C:\Users\Public\Pictures\Sample Pictures) when viewing files in Computer and Windows Explorer. Figure 5.11 shows the difference been XP and Vista.

1 Windows XP

2 Windows Vista

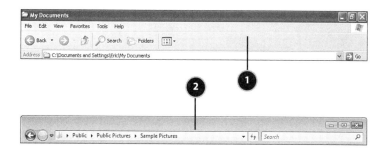

FIGURE 5.11

Address bars in Windows XP and Windows Vista.

As Figure 5.12 shows, Vista displays a breadcrumb navigation which is more user-friendly, however makes it more difficult to get to the raw path. Getting to the raw path is useful to those who copy and paste the path in other applications or for other miscellaneous uses.

Nevertheless, you can access the raw path by clicking on the right of the breadcrumb navigation, inside the Address bar, as demonstrated in Figure 5.12.

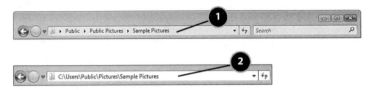

(1) Click here to show the raw path.

(2) The raw path is shown here.

FIGURE 5.12

Accessing the raw path.

The path will be highlighted and you can now copy and paste it as you want.

54 Up Arrow Has Been Removed

Among the other changes to Vista's new interface when viewing files with Computer or Windows Explorer is the removal of the Up button (see Figure 5.13) to quickly take you to the parent or previous folder.

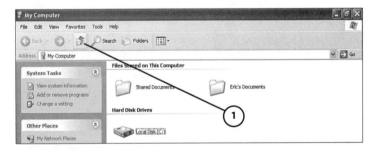

(1) The Up arrow in Windows XP

FIGURE 5.13

Using the up button to move back to the parent folder in Windows XP.

Similar functionality is given by clicking on the breadcrumb navigation links, such as demonstrated in Figure 5.14. Instead of clicking the Up arrow as you did in Windows XP, you simply click the actual folder name to navigate to that folder.

(1) Click the actual folder name.

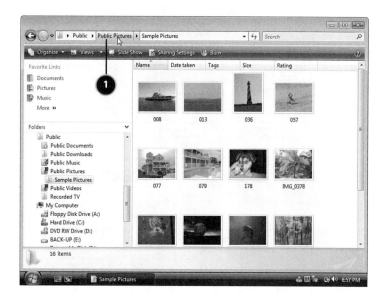

FIGURE 5.14

Clicking on the previous folder link to move back to the parent folder.

However, this new method of getting to the parent directory might not always be the best. For example, Figure 5.15 shows what happens when the Computer window is sized smaller; some of the breadcrumb navigation is lost, which prevents clicking on the parent link.

To overcome this problem, simply press Alt+↑ to navigate one level at a time. For instance, look at Figure 5.14. If I were to press Alt+↑, I would be taken to the Public Pictures folder. Pressing Alt+↑ again would take me to the Public folder.

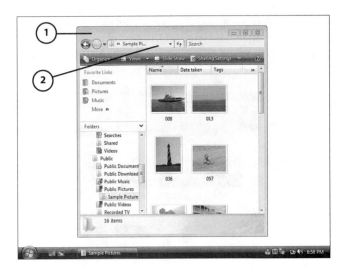

① When the Computer window is sized down…

② …some breadcrumb navigation links are not visible.

FIGURE 5.15

Example of how breadcrumb navigation links disappear when resizing.

55 My Network Places

The My Network Places feature found in Windows XP has been renamed simply to Network in Windows Vista. By default, a shortcut to your Network is on the Start menu, as you can see in Figure 5.16.

FIGURE 5.16

The Network icon on the Start menu.

> **🖥 TIP**
>
> Another neat enhancement to Windows Vista that you might be interested in is the Network Map. This offers a visual diagram of the network, including infrastructure components such as routers and user devices.
>
> To access the Network Map, open the Network and Sharing Center by right-clicking on the Network Status icon in the system tray, and click the View Full Map link in the upper-right corner.

TIP

You can also add a Network shortcut to your desktop. For more information, see #40, "Add the Main Icons."

You'll also find a shortcut for the Network in Windows Explorer and Computer, as shown in Figure 5.17.

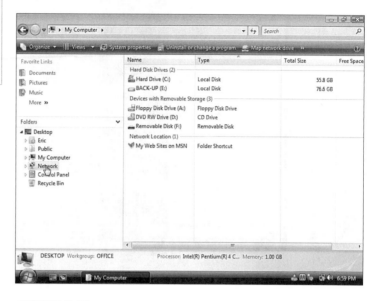

FIGURE 5.17

The Network icon in Windows Explorer.

FIGURE 5.18

Accessing the personalization settings from the desktop.

56 Desktop Settings

As you might recall, previous versions of Windows had a central location from which you could access your display, desktop, monitor, and other environment settings. This single window, called Display Properties, has been renamed and repurposed in Vista as a Control Panel applet called Personalization.

The easiest way to access the Personalization window is via the desktop:

1. Right-click on your desktop.

2. Select Personalize, as shown in Figure 5.18.

You can also access the Personalization window in Control Panel:

1. Open the Start menu.

2. Click Control Panel, as shown in Figure 5.19.

① Open the Start menu…

② …and then click Control Panel.

FIGURE 5.19

Opening Control Panel.

3. Double-click on the Personalization icon, as shown in Figure 5.20.

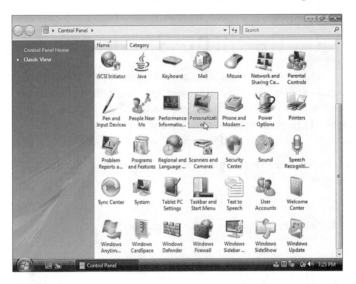

FIGURE 5.20

Accessing the personalization settings from Control Panel.

57 Advanced Performance Settings

In previous versions of Windows, you could the access advanced performance options, such as whether to smooth out edges of windows and other visual effects that involve the performance and appearance of Windows, from a tab on the System Properties window. The settings still are accessible from this window from within Vista, but you might find the Advanced Performance Options window itself difficult to find.

Here's how to get to the advanced performance options in Vista:

1. Right-click on the Computer icon. If the Computer icon isn't on the desktop, open the Start menu, click Control Panel, double-click on the System Settings icon, and proceed to the next step.

2. Select Properties, as shown in Figure 5.21.

3. Click the Advanced System Settings link, as shown in Figure 5.22, on the tasks pane.

 TIP

By default, the Computer icon isn't displayed on the desktop. If you want to add this icon to the desktop, see #40, "Add the Main Icons."

(**1**) Right-click the Computer icon…

(**2**) …and then click Properties.

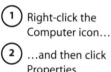

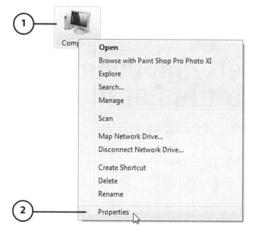

FIGURE 5.21

Accessing the system settings.

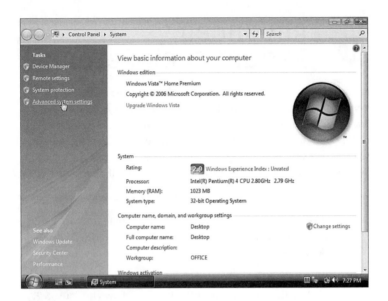

FIGURE 5.22

Accessing the advanced performance settings.

58 Network Connection Status Details

Viewing the details of your network connections (such as data rate and IP address information) in Windows Vista takes a few clicks—rather than the easy hovering-over or double-clicking the network status icon in the system tray as you could in XP.

In Vista, you access your network connection status details via the Network and Sharing Center. To access it:

1. Right-click on the Network Status icon in the system tray and select Network and Sharing Center, as shown in Figure 5.23.

2. Click the View Status link, as shown in Figure 5.24.

   For even more network details, such as the IP addresses, click the Details... button.

(1) Right-click on the
Network Status icon.

(2) Choose Network and
Sharing Center.

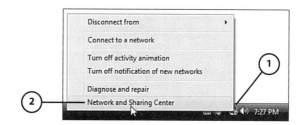

FIGURE 5.23

Opening the Network and Sharing Center.

(1) Click View Status to see
network details.

FIGURE 5.24

Accessing the connection details of the network connection.

59 Wireless Network Connection Priorities and Preferences

Just like the majority of the other networking tasks and preferences, to prioritize your wireless networks and to configure other individual settings (such as autoconnecting), you need to go to the Network and Sharing Center.

Here's how to access the individual settings and preferences of wireless networks:

1. Right-click on the Network Status icon in the system tray, and select Network and Sharing Center, as shown in Figure 5.25.

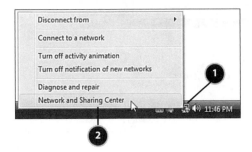

① Right-click on the taskbar.

② Choose Network and Sharing Center.

FIGURE 5.25

Opening the Network and Sharing Center.

2. Click the Manage Wireless Networks link, as shown in Figure 5.26, on the tasks pane.

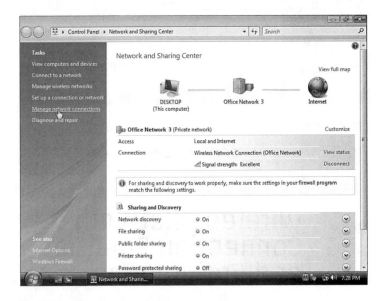

FIGURE 5.26

Opening the Manage Wireless Networks window.

3. To change the priority of the wireless networks, use the Move Up and Move Down arrows, which are shown in Figure 5.27. Prioritizing helps determine which network to use when there is more than one network in range.

1 Use the Move Up and Move Down arrows to set network priorities.

2 Double-click on a network to change its properties.

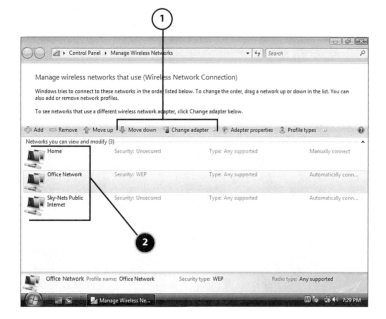

FIGURE 5.27

The arrow to change the position of the priority of a wireless network.

4. You can also double-click on a network to configure the properties of the individual wireless network connection. As Figure 5.28 shows, you can specify a few connectivity preferences and the connection's security settings, as shown in Figure 5.29.

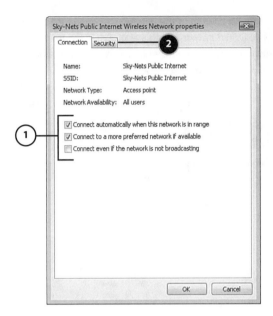

1. Set connectivity preferences here.

2. Find network security settings here.

FIGURE 5.28

Example of the connectivity preferences of a wireless network.

FIGURE 5.29

Example of the security settings of a wireless network.

60 Network Connections

Just as in the two previous topics, the Network Connections window can be accessed from the Network and Sharing Center. The Network Connections window displays all the network adapters and connections, such as PCI wireless cards and integrated network cards. This window also provides access to the network connection properties and diagnosis tools, and is where they can be turned on and off.

Here's how to access the Network Connections window:

1. Right-click on the Network Status icon in the system tray and select Network and Sharing Center, as shown in Figure 5.30.

(1) Right-click on the taskbar.

(2) Choose Network and Sharing Center.

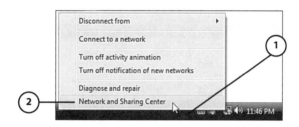

FIGURE 5.30

Opening the Network and Sharing Center.

2. Click the Manage Network Connections link, as shown in Figure 5.31, on the tasks pane.

Although the Network Connections window is only a few clicks away, Windows XP offered a Network Connections shortcut from the status icon in the system tray and from the Settings menu on the Start menu, which were a bit more convenient for regular network users. However, Windows Vista users can also get this icon on the Start menu if the Classic Start menu is enabled, which is discussed in #45, "Change to the Classic Start Menu."

You can also create a shortcut to Network Connections on your desktop:

1. Right-click on the desktop.

2. Point to New and click Shortcut, as shown in Figure 5.32.

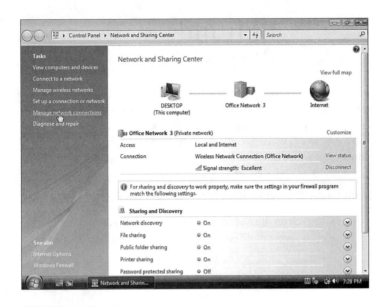

FIGURE 5.31

Opening the Network Connections window.

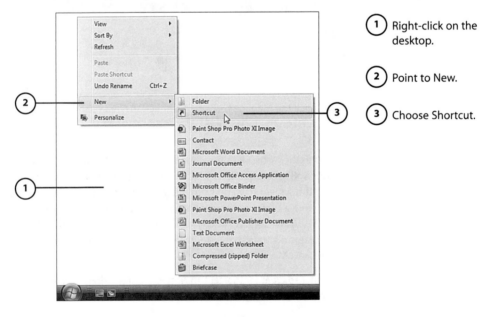

FIGURE 5.32

Creating a new shortcut.

3. Enter the following for the location, as shown in Figure 5.33:

C:\windows\system32\ncpa.cpl

(1) Enter the location in which you want the shortcut placed and click Next.

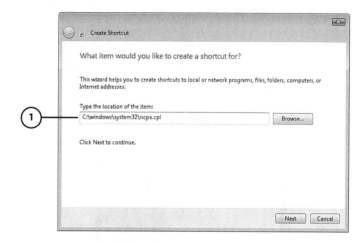

FIGURE 5.33

Entering a location for the new shortcut.

4. Click Next.

5. Enter a desired name, such as that shown in Figure 5.34, and click Finish.

(1) Enter a name for the newly created shortcut.

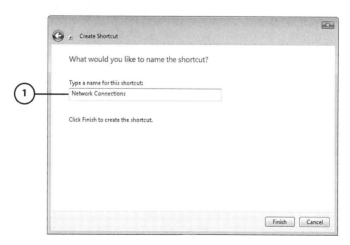

FIGURE 5.34

Entering a name for the new shortcut.

61 HyperTerminal

HyperTerminal was included with previous versions of Windows to provide command-prompt, text-only connections to other computers and hosts; however, it has been removed from Windows Vista. You can use Telnet, however.

By default, Telnet is not installed with Windows Vista, although you can install it by following these steps:

1. Open the Start menu.
2. Click Control Panel, as shown in Figure 5.35.

① Open the Start menu.

② Select Control Panel.

FIGURE 5.35

Opening Control Panel.

3. Click Programs and Features, as shown in Figure 5.36.
4. Click Turn Windows Features On or Off, as shown in Figure 5.37.

(1) Choose Programs and
Features.

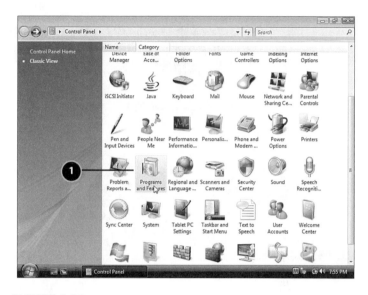

FIGURE 5.36

Accessing the Programs and Features section of Control Panel.

(1) Choose Turn Windows
Features On or Off.

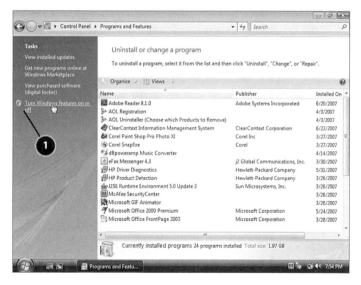

FIGURE 5.37

Accessing the Windows Features options.

5. In the Windows Features dialog box, check the Telnet Client
option, as shown in Figure 5.38, and then click OK.

① Choose Telnet Client.

FIGURE 5.38

Enabling the Telnet Client option.

After the Telnet Client is installed, you can use the program by browsing to and opening the file at C:\windows\system32\telnet.exe, or you can use Vista's new Search box on the Start menu:

1. Open the Start menu and type Telnet into the Search box, as shown in Figure 5.39.

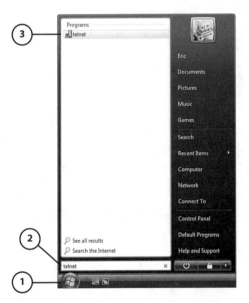

① Open the Start menu.

② Type telnet into the Search box and press Enter.

③ Telnet appears here; double-click to run it.

FIGURE 5.39

Accessing the Telnet application.

TIP

For a list of available commands in Telnet, simply type "?" and press Enter.

If using the Classic Start menu, you need to click Run, type C:\windows\system32\telnet.exe, and then click OK.

62 Run Prompt

The Run button that was accessible with a single click on the Start menu in other versions of Windows has been moved in Vista so that it appears in the Accessories folder. The Run prompt allows you to open files and folders by typing the exact path or to open other programs and tools by entering shortcuts, such as "msconfig."

Here are step-by-step directions to access the Run prompt in Vista:

1. Open the Start menu.
2. Click All Programs.
3. Click Accessories.
4. Click Run, as shown in Figure 5.40.

 TIP

If you enable the Classic Start menu, the Run button will return to the Start menu. For more information about this, see #45, "Change to the Classic Start Menu."

 TIP

Keep in mind that you can also use the new search capabilities of the Start menu to access many items you use with the Run prompt.

For example, you can either click on the Start button or press the Win key on your keyboard to access the Start menu, then you could type "msconfig" (without the quotes) and press Enter, just like you would have when using Run to open the System Configuration utility.

For more information about the new search capabilities, see #17, "New Look and Functionality."

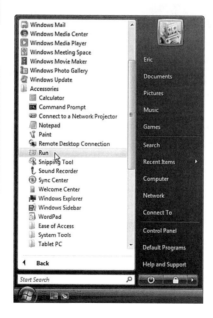

FIGURE 5.40

Opening the Run prompt.

63 System Restore

In Windows XP, you could change the System Restore settings via a tab on the System Properties window, accessed in Control Panel or by viewing the properties of My Computer. In Windows Vista, you can still access these settings from the System Properties window; however, the location of the settings isn't as obvious.

Here's how to get to the System Restore settings:

1. Right-click on the Computer icon and select Properties, as shown in Figure 5.41.

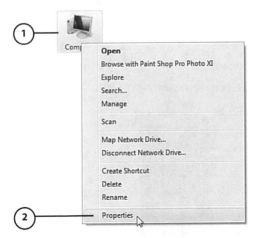

① Right-click the Computer icon.

② Choose Properties.

FIGURE 5.41

Accessing the system settings.

2. Click System Protection, as shown in Figure 5.42.

To open the actual System Restore program, where you can restore a hard drive, you can click the System Restore button on the System Protection window or go to Start, All Programs, Accessories, System Tools, and click System Restore, as shown in Figure 5.43, just like previous versions of Windows.

FIGURE 5.42

Accessing the System Protection settings.

① Open the Start menu.

② Choose All Programs, Accessories, System Tools, System Restore.

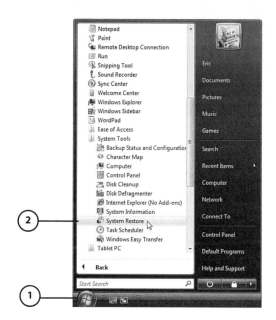

FIGURE 5.43

Opening the System Restore application.

64 Web Desktop Items

Previous versions of Windows contained a feature where you could place websites or web items on your desktop. Windows Vista, however, doesn't have this feature. Instead, you might want to use Windows Sidebar.

For more information on Windows Sidebar, see #17, "New Look and Functionality."

 TIP

You can use the Windows Sidebar to display the gadgets or you can detach them and place them on your desktop, which is similar to having the Web Desktop items in Windows XP.

65 Drag the Shortcut Icon in Microsoft Internet Explorer 7

With previous versions of Internet Explorer, you could create a shortcut for the particular website you're viewing by clicking and dragging the window's icon on the title bar in the upper-left corner, or the icon in the Address bar area to the desktop or other acceptable place.

However, with Internet Explorer 7, you can't use the icon in the title bar of the window, only the smaller icon directly to the left of the Address bar, as Figure 5.44 points out.

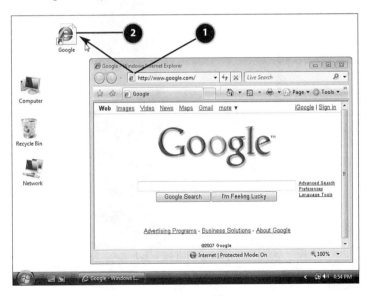

(1) Click this icon…

(2) …and drag it to the desired location.

FIGURE 5.44

Dragging an icon to create a shortcut of the current website.

66 Find On This Page in Internet Explorer 7

Although in Internet Explorer 7 you can still access the Find On This Page shortcut from the Edit menu, the menu bar isn't displayed by default. If you want, you can display the menu bar by pressing Alt on your keyboard or by right-clicking on the toolbar and selecting the Menu Bar option.

You can also search a page in Internet Explorer 7 by accessing the Find On This Page feature from the drop-down menu of the Search box, as shown in Figure 5.45.

 Click the down arrow.

 Choose Find On This Page.

TIP

You can also use the Alt key in most other Windows applications/windows to make the menu bar appear.

FIGURE 5.45

Accessing the Find On This Page feature.

67 View History in Internet Explorer 7

The History button (the clock with the green arrow found on the menu bar) has been removed from Internet Explorer 7. Internet Explorer 7, however, does offer a new button, as shown in Figure 5.46, which allows quick access to your Favorites, Feeds, and browsing History.

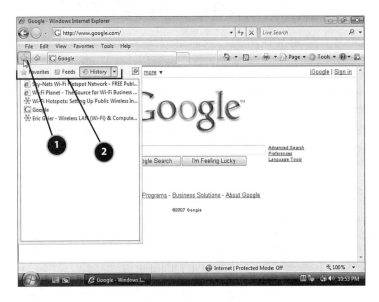

(1) Click the Favorites button.

(2) Choose one of these buttons.

FIGURE 5.46

Button to access the browsing history and other items.

With Internet Explorer 7, you can now search your browsing history (as shown in Figure 5.47) to make it even easier to find that previously viewed web page.

 CAUTION

Even though Internet Explorer's History feature is good for you when trying to find previously visited websites, remember other people using your Windows account can also see where you've been. To protect your privacy you can clear your history: In Internet Explorer 7, click the Tools button on the toolbar, select Delete Browsing History, and choose your desired option.

If you wish, you can even disable the History feature: In Internet Explorer 7, click the Tools button on the toolbar, select Internet Options, click the Settings button in the Browsing History section, and enter zero into the Days to keep pages in history field.

① Click the History button.

② Choose Search History.

③ Enter the URL and keyword for which you want to search.

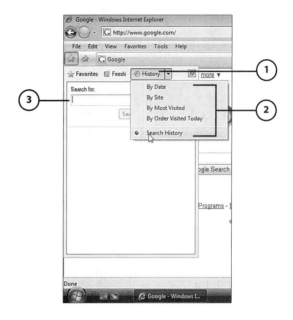

FIGURE 5.47

Example of searching through the browsing history.

68 Secure Website Padlock in Internet Explorer 7

As you might already know, Internet Explorer, like most web browsers, displays a padlock when viewing a secured website (such as banking sites) using the Secure Sockets Layer (SSL) security method. In previous versions of Internet Explorer, the padlock was shown in the lower-right corner of the browser window. In Internet Explorer 7, however, the padlock is shown toward the top of the browser on the right of the Address bar, as shown in Figure 5.48.

There have also been a few enhancements to this version of Internet Explorer to further improve the security and protection of your private information when using SSL-enabled websites. For example, when problems are found with a site's SSL certificate, Internet Explorer will display an alert page, such as the one shown in Figure 5.49, before loading the website.

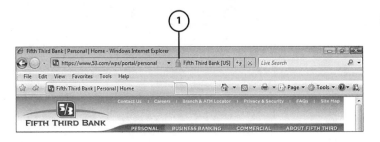

① Padlock icon indicates a security-enabled website.

FIGURE 5.48

New location of Internet Explorer's padlocks.

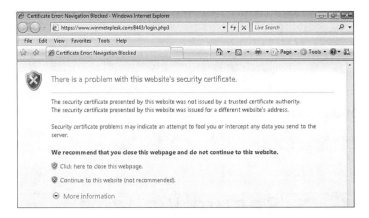

FIGURE 5.49

Example of an alert informing user of SSL certificate issues.

In addition, Internet Explorer now offers quick access to the SSL certificate details by clicking on the padlock, as shown in Figure 5.50.

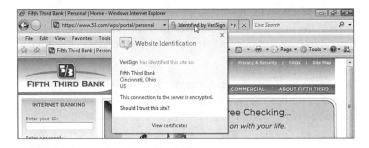

FIGURE 5.50

Accessing the SSL certificate details.

TIP

Another enhancement of Windows Vista is the ability to change the volume for each individual application.

See #99, "Adjust Audio Levels per Application," for more information.

69 Volume Control

In previous versions of Windows, you could access the Volume Control window by clicking Start, All Programs, Accessories, and Entertainment; however, in Vista there isn't an Entertainment folder. In addition, this window has been renamed Volume Mixer and now allows you to control the volume for each individual application.

Here's how to get to the new volume control utility, called Volume Mixer:

1. Right-click the Volume icon on the taskbar, as shown in Figure 5.51.
2. Select Open Volume Mixer.

① Right-click the Volume icon on the taskbar.

② Choose Open Volume Mixer.

FIGURE 5.51

Right-clicking on the Volume icon.

 TIP

To access advanced volume and sound settings, you can right-click on the Volume icon and select Sounds.

70 Add/Remove Programs

Need to uninstall a program? Can't find the Add/Remove utility? Well, it's still accessible from Control Panel, but it has been renamed to Programs and Features.

Here's how to get to the new Add/Remove utility, called Programs and Features:

1. Open the Start menu.
2. Click Control Panel, as shown in Figure 5.52.
3. Double-click on the Programs and Features icon, as shown in Figure 5.53.

① Open the Start menu.

② Select Control Panel.

FIGURE 5.52

Opening Control Panel.

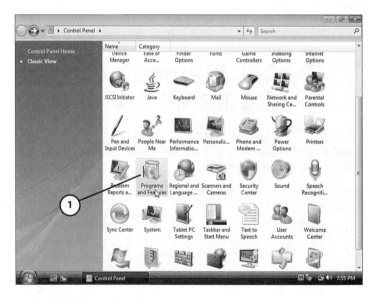

① Double-click Programs and Features.

> 🖳 **TIP**
>
> If you want to install or uninstall a Windows component, you can click on the Turn Windows Features On or Off link, located on the tasks pane of the Programs and Features window.

FIGURE 5.53

Accessing the Programs and Features section of Control Panel.

71 Display Properties

As you might recall, previous versions of Windows had a central place where you could access your display, desktop, monitor, and other environment settings. This single window, called Display Properties, has been manipulated in Windows Vista.

A main window called Personalization now exists in Vista. From this new window, you can access most of the old settings that were in the Display Properties window of previous versions of Windows.

The easiest way to access the Personalization window is via the desktop:

1. Right-click on your desktop.
2. Select Personalize, as shown in Figure 5.54.

① Right-click the desktop.

② Choose Personalize.

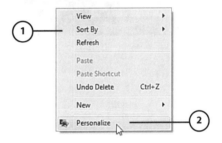

FIGURE 5.54

Accessing the personalization settings from the desktop.

You can also access the Personalization window from Control Panel:

1. Open the Start menu.
2. Click Control Panel, as shown in Figure 5.55.
3. Double-click on the Personalization icon, as shown in Figure 5.56.

1. Open the Start menu.

2. Select Control Panel.

FIGURE 5.55

Opening Control Panel.

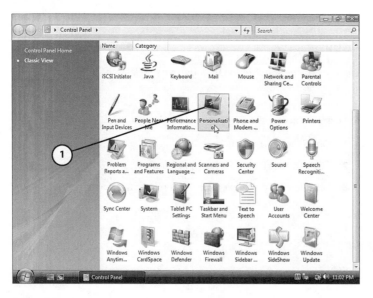

1. Choose the Personalization applet from Control Panel.

FIGURE 5.56

Accessing the personalization settings from Control Panel.

72 Filmstrip View

Many Windows XP users are fans of the Filmstrip view (as shown in Figure 5.57), which offers a very easy way to preview images and other documents without opening them directly.

(1) Select a thumbnail…

(2) …and see a larger version here.

(3) Flip forward or back through your image files.

(4) Rotate the image for onscreen viewing.

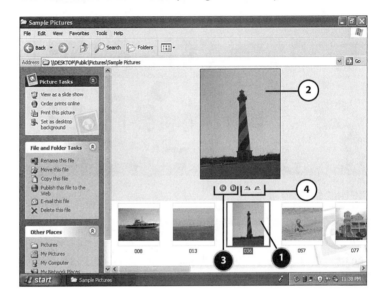

FIGURE 5.57

Example of viewing photos in Windows XP using the Filmstrip view.

Although Windows Vista doesn't have the Filmstrip view, it does offer similar views, which are fairly difficult to unearth if you don't know exactly what to look for.

First, you can try using the details pane, which is usually enabled by default. As Figure 5.58 shows, clicking on images in the Computer or Windows Explorer window shows the file's details and a view of the image in the details pane which is actually smaller than the thumbnail.

① Select an image.

② See a preview and the image properties here.

TIP

To enable the details pane in the Computer or Windows Explorer window, click the Organize button on the toolbar, select Layout, and then click the Details Pane option.

FIGURE 5.58

Example of using the details pane to preview photos.

The trick is to then resize the details pane to make it bigger, as shown in Figure 5.59, which will then be similar to the Filmstrip view offered in Windows XP.

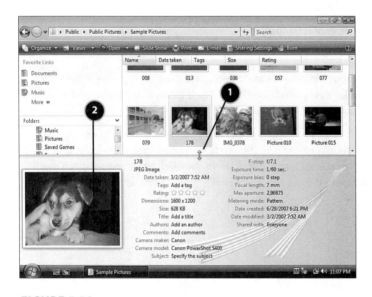

① Use the resizing handle to change the size of the details pane.

② The image preview will increase/decrease in size based on the relative size of the details pane.

FIGURE 5.59

Resizing the details pane to better view photos.

If that option doesn't float your boat, you can try using the preview pane:

1. In the Computer or Windows Explorer window, click the Organize button on the toolbar, as shown in Figure 5.60.

2. Select Layout, and click the Preview Pane option, as shown in Figure 5.61.

3. Then, you can resize the preview pane to your liking and get rid of the details pane if you choose.

FIGURE 5.60

Accessing the organization settings for the folder.

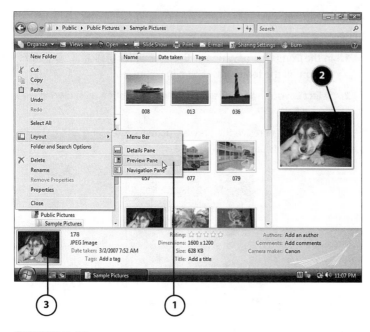

① Choose Organize, Layout, Preview Pane.

② The preview pane appears on the right.

③ Resize or remove the details pane if you want.

FIGURE 5.61

Enabling the preview pane for the folder.

6

Tips and Tricks

Want to do some neat things with Vista? Save time? Customize? Discover more? This chapter shows you many tips and tricks on Vista's new features and capabilities. You'll discover a very broad range of things you can do that will make your Windows Vista experience even better.

73 Apply the Vista Style to XP Computers

If you skipped Chapter 4, "Changing the Look and Feel of Vista," and are sticking with Vista's new interface, you might be interested in making other PCs running XP resemble Vista. Doing so might help you get used to the new interface, especially if you still regularly use your XP machines. In addition, flipping between the different Windows interfaces can be quite annoying. However, you can easily apply the Vista interface look and feel to your XP machines with some help from third-party programs, such as:

- Vista Transformation Pack:

   www.windowsxlive.net/index.php?page_id=15

- WindowBlinds:

   www.stardock.com/products/windowblinds

74 Display a Menu of Items on the Start Menu

Setting up some of the links and shortcuts on your Start menu to expand into a menu can save you from a few clicks here and there. For example, instead of clicking on the Computer shortcut and then having to click on the C drive, you can set up the Computer shortcut as a menu and then all you have to do is hover over the Computer shortcut on the Start menu and select the C drive. Figure 6.1 shows an example.

Here's how to display menus for links and shortcut items on the Start menu:

1. Right-click on the taskbar and select Properties, as shown in Figure 6.2.

① Clicking on Start menu
items with an arrow
opens a submenu
showing the contents
of that item.

② Submenu showing
contents of Computer

FIGURE 6.1

Example of menu option for Computer on the Start menu.

① Right-click on the
taskbar.

② Choose Properties.

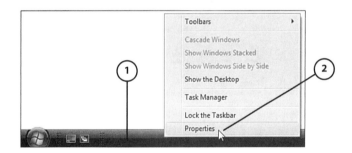

FIGURE 6.2

Opening Taskbar and Start Menu Properties.

 2. Select the Start Menu tab, as shown in Figure 6.3.

 3. Follow these steps if you're using the Classic Start Menu option:

 a. Click on the Customize button, as shown in Figure 6.4.

FIGURE 6.3

Selecting the Start Menu tab.

FIGURE 6.4

Opening the customization settings for the Classic Start menu style.

b. In the Advanced Start Menu Options section, as shown in Figure 6.5, check the items you want to be expanded as a menu. Vista allows you to expand Control Panel, Documents, Network Connections, Pictures, and Printers.

① Check the items you want to expand on the Start menu.

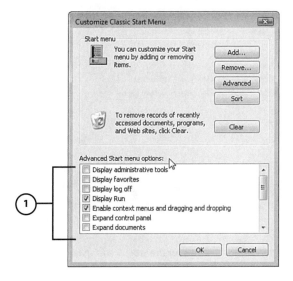

FIGURE 6.5

Customization settings for the Classic Start Menu style.

4. Follow these steps if you're using the Start Menu option:

a. Click on the Customize button, as shown in Figure 6.6.

b. Indicate which items you want to be expanded as a menu by checking the Display As a Menu option, as shown in Figure 6.7, on the appropriate item(s). Vista allows you to expand Control Panel, Documents, Network Connections, Pictures, and Printers.

5. Click OK.

FIGURE 6.6

Opening the customization settings for the Start Menu style.

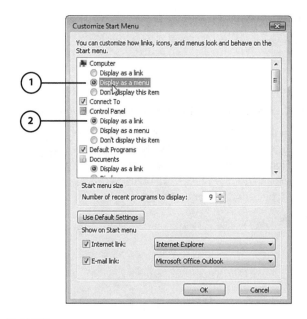

(1) Checking Display As Menu makes the Control Panel menu fly out from the Start menu.

(2) Checking Display As a Link makes the Control Panel window open.

FIGURE 6.7

Customization settings for the Start Menu style.

75 Add More Gadgets to Sidebar

As you might have read in #17, "New Look and Functionality," Windows Vista's Sidebar feature can be a convenient and time-saving tool. However, to get the most out of it, you should explore all the gadgets and ensure it's customized to your lifestyle and liking.

Here's how to add gadgets to Windows Sidebar:

1. Either right-click on the Windows Sidebar and select Add Gadgets, as shown in Figure 6.8, or simply click the Add button on the top of the Sidebar, as shown in Figure 6.9.

 Right-click on the Sidebar.

 Choose Add Gadgets.

 Click the Add button on the Sidebar to add gadgets.

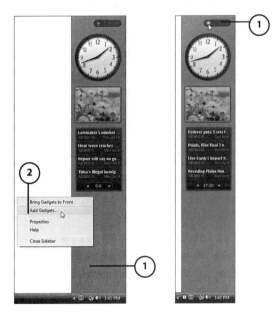

FIGURE 6.8

Opening the Gadget browser.

FIGURE 6.9

Opening the Gadget browser.

> **TIP**
>
> Windows Sidebar is set by default to automatically appear when you start Windows Vista. If you've closed it, however, don't worry. You can open Windows Sidebar by opening the Start menu, pointing to All Programs, pointing to Accessories, and then clicking Windows Sidebar.
>
> If you've also disabled it from automatically appearing when you start Windows and you've now changed your mind, you easily reenable this by right-clicking on Windows Sidebar, selecting Properties, and checking the Start Sidebar When Windows Starts option on the top.

2. Then, you'll see all the installed gadgets, which include those from Microsoft (as Figure 6.10 shows) that are preloaded with Windows Vista.

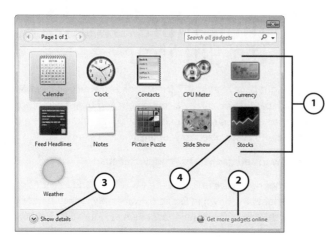

1. Preloaded Windows gadgets

2. Click here to get more gadgets.

3. Click Show Details to learn more about the selected gadget.

4. Drag gadgets to the Sidebar or desktop to use them.

FIGURE 6.10

The Windows Sidebar Gadget browser.

Either double-click on a gadget to add it to the Sidebar, or click on a gadget and drag it anywhere on your desktop or the Sidebar. Keep in mind, dragging gadgets from the Sidebar or directly from the gadget window and placing them somewhere on your desktop typically makes the gadget larger and offers more features. For example, when the weather gadget is on the Sidebar, it only shows the temperature, however, when placed on the desktop, it displays the three-day forecast.

76 Change Power Button on Start Menu

By default, the Power button on your Start menu is set to put your PC in Sleep mode. Though this might be fine for some, you might want the Power button to simply shut down your PC. For example, if you usually choose to shut down your PC instead of putting it into Sleep mode, then you're likely aware that it takes an added click to the arrow on the Start menu to shut down your PC. In other words, it's a waste of time. Reconfiguring the Start menu Power button shaves a few seconds off the usual process.

Here's how to change the setting for your Start menu Power button:

1. Open the Start menu and select Control Panel.

2. Double-click on Power Options.

TIP

Don't limit yourself to the few gadgets Microsoft offers; there are thousands of gadgets out there!

To view Microsoft's listing of third-party gadgets, click the Get More Gadgets Online button in the lower-right corner of the gadget window. You can also search the web for even more gadgets.

TIP

If you don't like the Sidebar always taking up space on your screen, you can either close Windows Sidebar (by right-clicking on it and selecting Close Sidebar) and keep any gadgets on your desktop, or you can stop the Sidebar from appearing in front of other windows (by right-clicking on the Sidebar, selecting Properties, and unchecking the Sidebar is Always on Top of Other windows option), which makes it only accessible when viewing your desktop.

3. Click the Choose What the Power Button Does link, as shown in Figure 6.11, in the tasks pane.

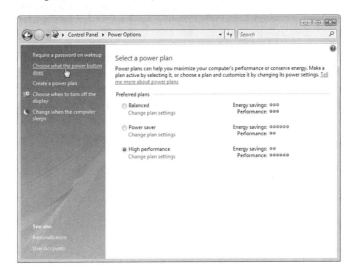

FIGURE 6.11

Opening the System Power Options.

> **TIP**
>
> You might also be interested in getting back the Log Off button (which was a staple in Windows XP). If so, see #46, "Display the Log Off Button on the Start Menu."

4. In the Power Button Settings area, as shown in Figure 6.12, choose either Do Nothing, Sleep, or Shut Down from the drop-down list.

5. Click Save Settings.

(1) Click this drop-down menu…

(2) …and choose what action Vista should take when the Power button is clicked.

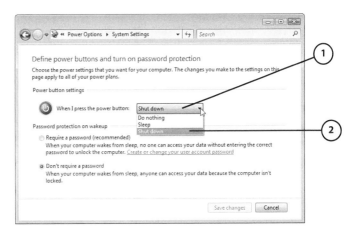

FIGURE 6.12

Selecting the Power button option.

77 Set Up Additional Clocks for Other Time Zones

Windows Vista allows you to set up two additional clocks, which can be very useful if you need to regularly reference the time from another zone. For example, you might set up an additional clock for a place you frequently visit or call.

Here's how to set up an additional clock:

1. Click on the time, as shown in Figure 6.13, in the lower-right corner of Vista.

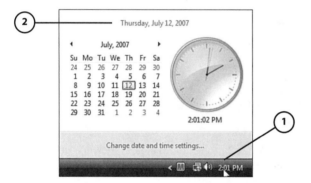

1 Click the clock on the taskbar.

2 From this window, choose Change Date and Time Settings.

FIGURE 6.13

Bringing up the clock and calendar.

2. Click on the Change Date and Time Settings link.

3. Select the Additional Clocks tab.

4. Check one of the Show This Clock boxes, as shown in Figure 6.14.

5. Using the drop-down menu, select the desired time zone for the clock, enter your preferred display name for the clock in the appropriate box, and click OK.

After you set up another clock, you can see the time by hovering over the clock, as shown in Figure 6.15, in the lower-right corner of Vista.

You can also click on the clock to view the actual clocks with the calendar.

① Click Show This Clock to add another clock to the desktop.

② Choose the time zone for the new clock.

③ Name the clock.

④ Click Show This Clock to add yet another clock if desired.

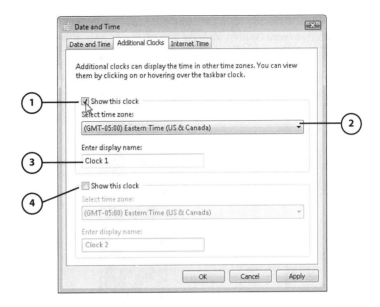

FIGURE 6.14

Setting up an additional clock.

① Hover your mouse over the clock on the taskbar.

② Times for all clocks you've set up appear.

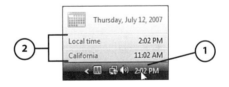

FIGURE 6.15

Viewing the additional clocks.

78 Use Military Time Format for the Clock

Are you (or were you) in the service and now the military time format is embedded in your head? Or, do you simply prefer the 24-hour time format? Well, you actually can change the default format to the 24-hour format so that 2:30 p.m. shows as 14:30.

Here's how to do it:

1. Click Start and type "intl.cpl" in the Search box, as shown in Figure 6.16, and then press Enter. If you're using the Classic Start

menu and the Search box is missing, you can open the Regional
and Language Options from Control Panel and proceed to the
next step.

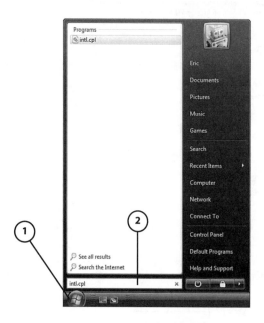

(1) Click Start.

(2) Type "intl.cpl" in the
Search box and press
Enter.

FIGURE 6.16

Opening the Regional and Language Options.

2. Click the Customize This Format button, as shown in Figure 6.17.

3. Click the Time tab.

4. Change the Time Format field to H:mm:ss, as shown in
Figure 6.18.

5. Click OK to apply the changes.

TIP

You can also change the
date format while you're
here. Simply click the Date
tab and make the changes.

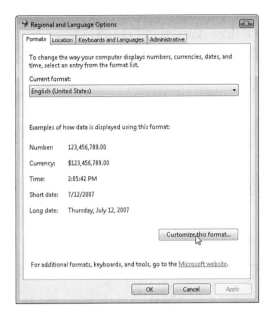

FIGURE 6.17

Opening the customization settings.

1. Choose the Time tab.

2. Change the Time Format field to H:mm:ss.

3. Click Reset to go back to default date and time settings.

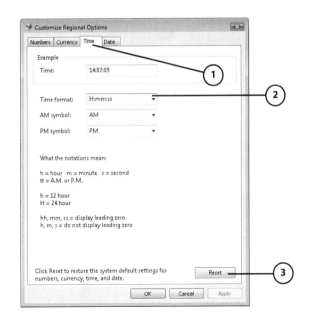

FIGURE 6.18

Example of correct Time Format to use military time.

79 Use the Taskbar Address Bar

Here's a shortcut for the surfing addicts. Although it's not a new feature to this version of Windows, you can add an Address bar to your Windows taskbar. This provides even quicker access to the Internet, taking advantage of today's high-speed, always-on connections to the Internet.

All you'll have to do is type an address in, press Enter, and then up pops the browser to the site you requested.

Here's how to add the Address bar to your Windows taskbar:

1. Right-click on the taskbar.

2. Click Toolbars, Address, as shown in Figure 6.19.

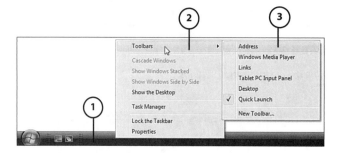

FIGURE 6.19

Enabling the Address bar on the Taskbar.

Now you can move and resize the Address bar by clicking on Address and dragging it to your desired location or size. Figure 6.20 shows an example.

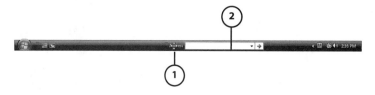

FIGURE 6.20

Example of moving the Address bar.

(1) Right-click on the taskbar.

(2) Choose Toolbars…

(3) …then select Address.

 TIP

In case you didn't already know, you can move and/or resize the Address bar. To do so, you first need to unlock the taskbar by right-clicking on the taskbar and selecting Lock the Taskbar.

(1) Use the move handle to place the Address bar wherever you prefer on the taskbar.

(2) Resize the Address bar simply by clicking and dragging.

To make more space on the Windows taskbar for open applications and windows to appear, you can expand your taskbar to two rows. To expand the taskbar, hover over the top edge so that the resize arrow appears and then drag to your desired size. Then, you could move the Address bar and other toolbars (such as the Quick Launch toolbar) to the bottom, leaving the top for application and window tabs. See Figure 6.21 for an example.

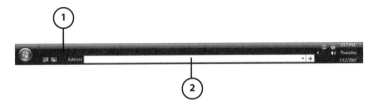

(1) Resize the taskbar by clicking the top edge and dragging upward.

(2) Move the Address bar to the bottom row of the taskbar.

FIGURE 6.21

Example of improved taskbar.

After you're done customizing your Windows taskbar, you should lock it again to prevent unintentional changes. To do this, right-click on the taskbar and select Lock the Taskbar.

80 Resize Icons with the Mouse

Windows Vista has three different default desktop icon sizes to choose from: Large, Medium, and Classic. As shown in Figure 6.22, you can change between these sizes by right-clicking on the desktop, choosing View, and then selecting the desired icon size.

(1) Right-click the desktop.

(2) Choose View.

(3) Select Large Icons, Medium Icons, or Classic Icons.

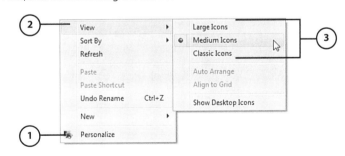

FIGURE 6.22

Changing the icon size using predefined sizes.

These aren't the only options you have, though. You can basically make your own size, as shown in Figure 6.23, from very small to very large.

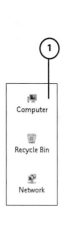

① Custom icons made very small

② Custom icons made very large

FIGURE 6.23

Vista allows you to choose your own custom icon size—from very small to very large.

Just having a choice between three different desktop icon sizes is an improvement from Windows XP, which only had one real default size and—if you were lucky enough to find it buried in the desktop effects preferences—a setting for larger icons. However, if you have a mouse with a scrolling wheel, Vista allows you to get exactly the size that's right for you.

Here's how to do it:

1. Simply click on your desktop or Computer/Windows Explorer.

2. Hold down the Ctrl key on your keyboard.

3. Scroll your mouse's wheel forward and back to change the size of the icons.

This feature wasn't only created to have some fun and play pranks on people (though it is good for that). It was created to help those with eyesight problems as well as appease those who prefer a minimalist

 TIP

You can also use the scrolling wheel on your mouse with Flip 3D. You can activate Flip 3D by pressing the Windows logo key+Tab and then using the wheel to flip through the windows instead of pressing the Tab key or keyboard arrow.

For more information about this feature refer to #94, "Change Windows Using Flip 3D."

approach to desktop organization. It's also useful for sizing thumbnail icons when viewing photos in Thumbnails view.

81 Search from the Start Menu

As discussed in #17, "New Look and Functionality," Vista contains a new search capability on the Start menu.

Here's how to search:

1. Simply open the Start menu and begin typing. As seen in Figure 6.24, the Start menu changes to show the best possible results.

The results will be sorted with the most frequently opened items on top. The more you type, the narrower the results. This way, you don't always have to type the entire name before finding what you want.

By default, the Search function will search communications (email messages, saved instant messages, appointments, and contacts), web favorites and history, user files (personal folders), and programs. If you want, you can disable any of these main search categories and you can choose to search the entire file index rather than just the user files.

> ## TIP
>
> The Search box is included on the Start menu by default; however, if you cannot locate it, it's likely because you've disabled it or have chosen the Classic Start menu.
>
> To change the Search box settings, right-click on the taskbar, click Properties, and click the Start Menu tab. Ensure the Start Menu option is checked, click the Customize button, and make sure the Search option is marked.

1. Click Start.

2. Type what you want to search for here.

3. The results appear here; double-click the one you want to open.

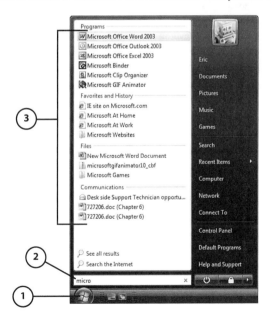

FIGURE 6.24

Example of using the Start menu's search capabilities.

Here's how to access the search preferences:

1. Right-click on the taskbar and select Properties.
2. Click the Start Menu tab.
3. Click the Customize button next to the Start Menu option.
4. Scroll down to see the search options, as shown in Figure 6.25.
5. Make your desired changes and click OK to exit.

By default, the Indexed locations (meaning the places Windows tracks and includes in your search results) include your personal folder, email, and Start menu. You can, however, include other folders in the index, for inclusion in the Start menu search. For example, by default, files and folders stored in other locations than the ones detailed previously (that is, C:\Vacation Photos\) won't appear in the searches. However, you can add any location to the index.

 TIP

Keep in mind that you can also use the new search capabilities of the Start menu to access many items you use with the Run prompt.

For example, you could simply type "msconfig" (without the quotes) into the Start menu Search box and press Enter, rather than accessing the Run prompt, which is now located in the Accessories submenu of the Start menu.

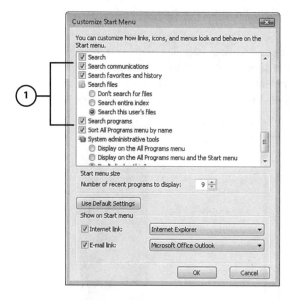

① Choose what items Windows should search.

FIGURE 6.25

Search options for Start menu.

Here's how to add folders to the search index:

1. Open the Start menu.
2. Click Control Panel.
3. Double-click on the Indexing Options icon.
4. Click Modify, as shown in Figure 6.26.

(1) Currently indexed—or searchable—locations are shown here.

(2) Choose Modify to add or remove search locations.

(3) Click here to learn more about indexing and how it affects your searches.

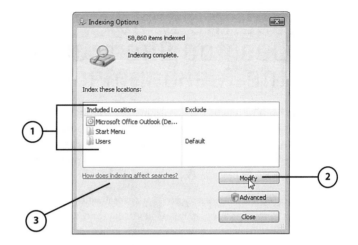

FIGURE 6.26

Accessing the Indexing settings.

5. Click the Show All Locations button.

6. Browse through the locations using the arrows to expand the folders. Select folders to include in the index by marking its check box. Figure 6.27 shows an example.

7. When you are finished, click OK to exit.

(1) Click Show All Locations to see a listing of all possible search locations.

(2) All possible search locations appear in a scrollable list; choose the ones you want indexed.

(3) See a summary of the indexed locations here.

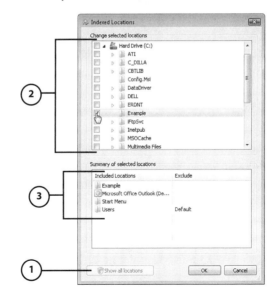

FIGURE 6.27

Example of adding a folder to be indexed.

82 Use the Show Desktop Shortcut on the Taskbar Menu

You might have been fortunate enough to discover the Show Desktop shortcut in Windows XP. For those who weren't, using this shortcut will save a great deal of clicks (and essentially time) on the Minimize button to reveal the desktop. This is especially true for those who multitask and have many windows and programs open at once.

For example, clicking the Minimize button for several windows and/or programs to get to the desktop can take an extra five seconds. Suppose you do this six times a day; you waste 30 seconds a day, and over three hours each year! Using the Show Desktop shortcut takes you directly to the desktop and doesn't waste any time. There are two ways to access this shortcut:

 TIP

If the Quick Launch toolbar is missing, you can enable it by right-clicking on the Taskbar, selecting Toolbars, and clicking Quick Launch.

- Click on the Show Desktop icon, as shown in Figure 6.28, in the Quick Launch toolbar.

- Right-click on the Taskbar and click Show the Desktop (also shown in Figure 6.28).

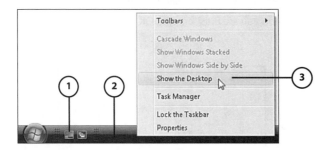

(1) Click the Show Desktop icon in the taskbar.

(2) Or, right-click the taskbar and…

(3) …choose Show the Desktop.

FIGURE 6.28

Showing the desktop.

83 Create a Shortcut to Network Connections

Although the new Network and Sharing Center might be great for the average consumer, it can be quite a nuisance for advanced users because of the added steps to access many of the networking configuration settings. Although Windows XP's networking area didn't offer an exceptionally user-friendly interface, it was quick and easy to access certain network settings if you knew what you were looking for.

For example, disabling or enabling a connection only took a right-click on the Network Status icon in the system tray; however, in Vista you have to open the Network and Sharing Center, click on a link to open the Network Connections window, and then you can disable/enable a connection.

To save a few clicks each time you need to manage your network connections, you can create a desktop shortcut directly to the Network Connections window; here's how:

1. Right-click on the desktop, point to New, and then click Shortcut.

2. In the location field, enter the following (as shown in Figure 6.29):

   explorer.exe ::{7007ACC7-3202-11D1-AAD2-00805FC1270E}

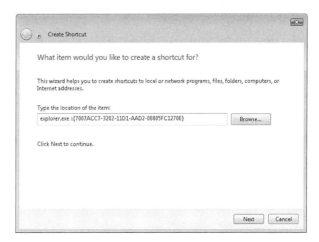

FIGURE 6.29

Entering the shortcut location.

3. After clicking Next, enter a name for the shortcut, as shown in Figure 6.30, and then click Finish.

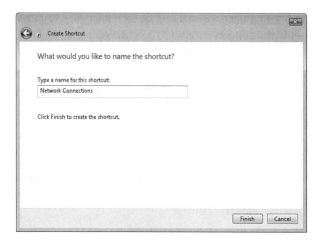

FIGURE 6.30

Entering a shortcut name.

If you want, you can even apply the Network Connections icon to the shortcut. Here's how:

1. Right-click the icon and select Properties.

2. Click the Change Icon button.

3. Enter the following into the text field (as shown in Figure 6.31):

    %SystemRoot%\system32\netshell.dll

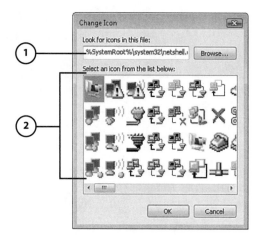

① Choose the location to search for icons here.

② Choose the icon you want to use from the ones appearing here.

FIGURE 6.31

Specifying the icon location.

TIP

For even quicker access to the Network Connections window, you can add the icon to the Quick Launch toolbar. Just drag the new desktop icon and drop it into the Quick Launch area.

4. Click OK to select the icon and click OK on the shortcut properties window to exit and apply the changes.

84 Restart the Windows Explorer Shell Without Rebooting Windows

Like most Windows users, you've probably encountered the occasional freeze-up when working with a Windows component (such as Windows Explorer or the desktop), rather than a specific application. Often, your only recourse seems to be to reboot the PC, losing any unsaved data in open programs. However, there's a way to fix this type of problem without rebooting and losing your work:

1. When a Windows component freezes and becomes unresponsive, press Ctrl+Alt+Del.

2. Click the Start Task Manager button, as shown in Figure 6.32.

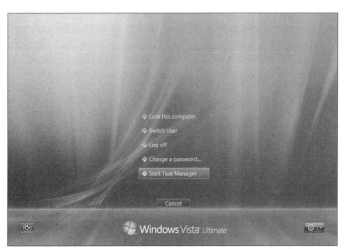

FIGURE 6.32

Opening Task Manager.

3. Click the Processes tab.

4. In the Image Name column, find the explorer.exe process.

5. Right-click on explorer.exe and select End Process, as shown in Figure 6.33.

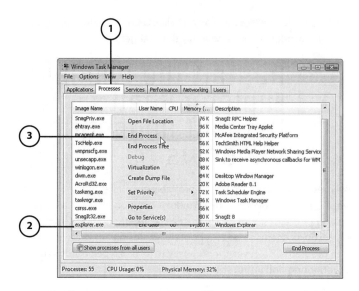

① Click the Processes tab.

② Right-click on explorer.exe.

③ Choose End Process.

FIGURE 6.33

Ending the Explorer process.

6. A Task Manager warning pop-up is displayed asking you to confirm that you really want to end the process. Click Yes to end the process, which should make the desktop, and possibly open applications, temporarily disappear.

7. In Task Manager, which should still be open, click on the File menu, and select New Task (Run...), as shown in Figure 6.34.

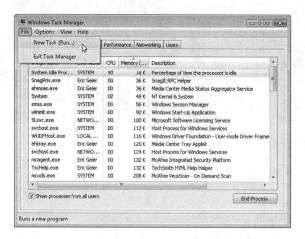

FIGURE 6.34

Starting a new task.

8. Type explorer.exe, as shown in Figure 6.35, and click OK. The Windows Explorer Shell restarts and should make the desktop, along with applications you had open, reappear.

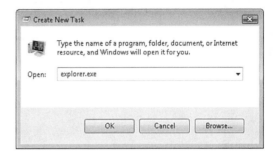

FIGURE 6.35

Opening Explorer.

85 View List of Shared Files and Folders

An exceptional improvement in the networking features of Windows Vista is the ability to easily and quickly see all the folders you're sharing. It's very easy to forget which folders you've shared over time. Vista, however, enables you to always know exactly what is being shared and to whom. Therefore, you can better protect your data and privacy, which is particularly important for those who often use untrusted networks such as Wi-Fi hot spots.

Here's how to view the lists of shared files and folders:

1. Right-click on the Network Status icon in the system tray, and select Network and Sharing Center.

2. Scroll all the way to the bottom of the Network and Sharing Center.

3. To view the files and folders you are sharing, click on the Show Me All the Files and Folders I Am Sharing and Show Me All the Shared Network Folders on This Computer links, as pointed out in Figure 6.36.

 TIP

It's a good idea to periodically check your shared folders, their permission settings, and their contents to make sure you don't unintentionally share something that's private or sensitive.

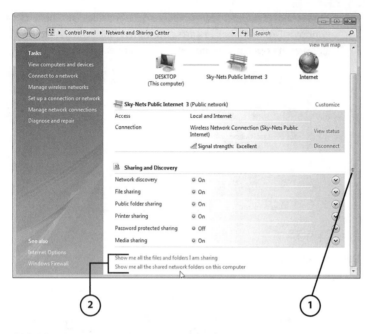

① Scroll to the bottom of the Network and Sharing Center.

② Choose these links to see all of the shared folders on your computer.

FIGURE 6.36

The links to view your shared resources.

86 Select Files Using Check Boxes

Have you ever been selecting multiple files by holding down the Ctrl key, you accidentally press or click something, and—BAM!—all the files open? (It happens to me at least once a month!) Well, you'll be thankful for the new check box feature (which you can see in Figure 6.37), and if you've been fortunate enough to not have experienced this yet, you might not ever if you use the check boxes to select files.

Here's how to enable the check box feature:

1. Open Computer, either via the Start menu or the desktop icon.

2. Click the Organize button and select Folder and Search Options, as shown in Figure 6.38.

① Vista's new check boxes allow you to select multiple files simply by clicking check boxes instead of Ctrl-clicking as you had to do in XP.

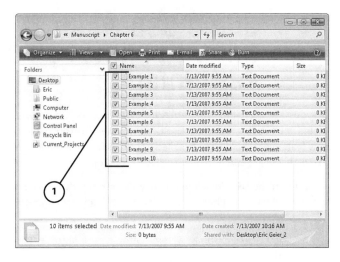

FIGURE 6.37

Example of the new check box feature.

① From Computer, choose Organize…

② …and then select Folder and Search Options.

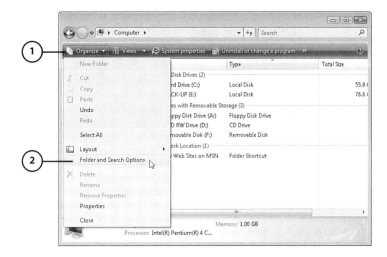

FIGURE 6.38

Opening the Folder and Search Options.

3. Click the View tab.

4. Scroll down and mark the Use Check Boxes to Select Items option.

87 Use a USB Flash Drive to Improve PC Performance

Do you have a USB flash (thumb) drive that has some spare space? Would you like to speed up your PC? (Who doesn't?) You're in luck, a new feature of Windows Vista called Windows ReadyBoost allows you to use that spare space to do just that—speed up your computer!

1. Insert the USB drive into one of your computer's USB ports. The AutoPlay dialog box opens a few seconds after plugging the drive in.

2. Click the Speed Up My System button on the AutoPlay window, as shown in Figure 6.39.

FIGURE 6.39

Opening the Windows ReadyBoost feature.

If the AutoPlay window doesn't open, you can access the same location by opening Computer or Windows Explorer, right-clicking on the device drive, selecting Properties, and clicking on the ReadyBoost tab. Then, you can proceed to the next step.

3. Select the Use This Device option, as shown in Figure 6.40.

4. By using the slider bar or typing into the field, choose how much space you want to dedicate to Windows ReadyBoost.

(1) Select Use This Device.

(2) Use the slider to tell
Vista how much of the
drive you want to use,
or…

(3) …type in a specific
number of MB you
want to use here.

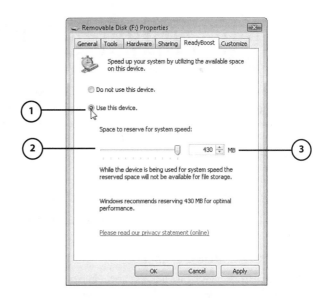

FIGURE 6.40

Enabling Windows ReadyBoost on the device.

5. Click OK to apply the changes and exit.

The space you specified will now be reserved for Windows
ReadyBoost, which is represented by a cache file called
ReadyBoost, as shown in Figure 6.41.

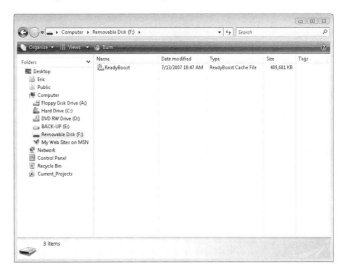

FIGURE 6.41

Example of the ReadyBoost cache file.

88 Refresh Your PC with a Nightly Reboot

Sometimes your PC needs a reboot to freshen up, which can help prevent lock ups and other performance issues and annoyances. However, like many others, you're probably not in the habit of regularly rebooting or shutting down your PC. A simple solution is to set up a nightly reboot. Therefore, it will automatically refresh every day, while not taking away from your computing time.

Follow these steps to set up a scheduled reboot:

1. Open the Start menu, and then open Task Scheduler by following this path:

   All Programs, Accessories, System Tools, Task Scheduler

2. Click on the Create Basic Task link, as shown in Figure 6.42, in the action pane on the right.

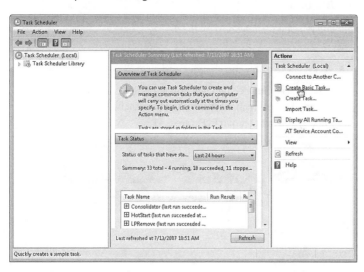

FIGURE 6.42

Creating a new task.

3. Enter a desired name and description, such as that shown in Figure 6.43, and click Next.

4. Choose the desired frequency, and then click Next.

① Name the task here.

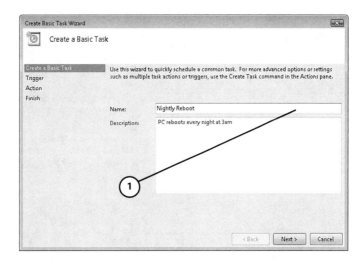

FIGURE 6.43

Entering task name and description.

5. Set the frequency preferences, as shown in Figure 6.44. You can choose a start date and time, then set how often this task should recur automatically. Then click Next.

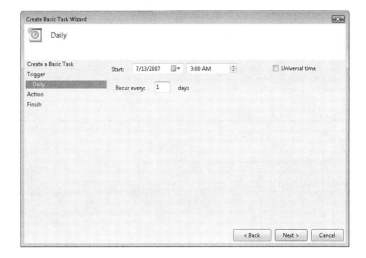

FIGURE 6.44

Setting the frequency preferences for the task.

6. Select the Start a Program option, as shown in Figure 6.45, and click Next.

FIGURE 6.45

Choosing the Start a Program task action.

7. In the Program/scripts field, enter the following:

   %SystemRoot%\System32\shutdown.exe

8. In the Add Arguments field, enter "–r", which tells Vista to reboot (see Figure 6.46).

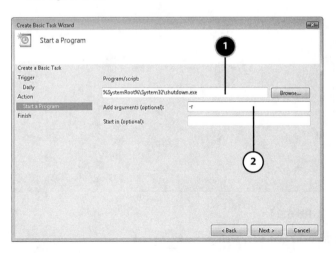

FIGURE 6.46

Specifying the script and argument settings for the task.

> **CAUTION**
>
> You should be careful when working with scripting, as mistakes can cause problems. Follow these directions carefully.
>
> If you want to learn more about scripting, you can refer to another book, such as *Windows Vista Guide to Scripting, Automation, and Command Line Tools* by Brian Knittel (Que, forthcoming).

① Enter a program or script here.

② Enter optional arguments here.

TIP

You can also specify more arguments in addition to the –r, which tells it to reboot. Here are a few more arguments you could use:

-t: Tells it to wait a certain amount of seconds until it reboots.

-c: Lets you add a comment that pops up when the task is run.

-g: Used in place of –r. The only difference is that this option will open the applications that were running before the restart, after the scheduled restart.

Here's an example of how these arguments would be typed in the Add Arguments field:

```
"-g -t 120 -c "Auto
restart in 2
minutes...""
```

TIP

You can easily test out the new task by running the Task Scheduler program and clicking on the Task Scheduler Library folder in the left tasks pane. Right-click on the new task and click Run.

If the new task doesn't appear in the Task Scheduler Library, you should click Action from the File menu at the top of the Task Scheduler program and choose Refresh.

9. Click Next to proceed.

10. Review the task properties and click Finish to create the new task.

To ensure you don't lose any work, you should save any open documents and close all applications before the reboot task runs.

89 Disable User Account Control Pop-up Alerts

As you perhaps have already found out, by default Windows Vista notifies you (see Figure 6.47 for an example) when certain areas that contain system settings are accessed. These pop-up alerts, however, can be annoying especially if you access these areas on a regular basis. The good news is that you can easily disable the User Account Control (UAC) and get rid of the alerts.

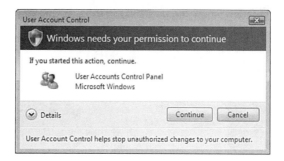

FIGURE 6.47

Example of a UAC alert.

Before you disable UAC, you should understand the risks involved, just as you should before disabling any type of security feature. You might think: "Why do I even need these alerts asking if I authorized the access of a certain area when I'm the one who told the computer to access it in the first place?" The answer is that the alerts notify you that you're performing an action that could put your computer at risk. More important, UAC sounds the alarm in case your computer has been breached by a hacker, virus, or other Internet nasty. Therefore, when disabling this feature, you are exposing your computer to some additional risk, though typically minimal. The bottom line is that you should not disable UAC unless you are aware of the risks and are comfortable taking those risks. It is not recommended for beginners to disable UAC.

A useful feature of the UAC pop-ups is that other nonadministrator Windows accounts (such as an account you would set up for your children or other family members using your PC) can't access areas protected by the UAC pop-ups. When a UAC pop-up appears on a nonadministrator Windows account, a password for an administrator must be given before access to the area is authorized. This is a great feature if you have children or others whom you don't want to be able to change system settings. If you still want to disable the alerts for yourself (and any other Administrator accounts), but keep it active for other users, see #90, "Disable UAC Pop-up Alerts for Only Administrators," rather than continuing with this one.

To disable UAC for all users:

1. Open the Start menu and select Control Panel.

2. Double-click User Accounts.

3. Click the Turn User Account Control On or Off link, as shown in Figure 6.48.

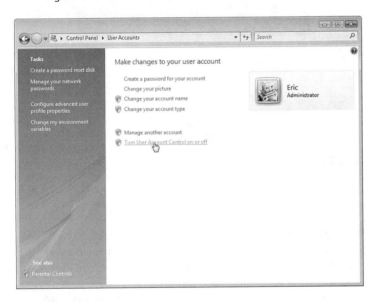

FIGURE 6.48

Accessing UAC settings.

4. Uncheck the Use User Account Control (UAC) to Help Protect Your Computer check box, as shown in Figure 6.49, and click OK.

FIGURE 6.49

Turning off the UAC feature and alerts.

 CAUTION

Be very careful when editing your Windows Registry. Mistakes could cause major problems, including making your PC unbootable. Before making any changes to the Registry, make sure you back it up first.

1. Open the Registry Editor by following steps 1 and 2.

2. In the Registry Editor, click File on the menu and select Export.

3. On the bottom of the dialog box, select the All option for the Export Range.

4. Browse, find, and select a location to save the registry. It's best to save it to a removable storage device like a flash drive, floppy disc, or CD.

5. Enter your desired file name, such as Registry_ Backup_*DATE*.

6. Click Save and wait until it's done which may take a few minutes.

5. A pop-up should appear stating a restart is required to apply the changes. Specify whether to restart now or later. UAC alerts will continue to appear until you restart.

90 Disable UAC Pop-up Alerts for Only Administrators

As mentioned in the preceding topic, you can disable the UAC pop-up alerts for Windows account administrators while keeping them active for other accounts, which is useful if you have children or other non-techies you don't want to have access to system settings. Disabling the alerts for specific users, however, requires editing the Windows Registry.

1. In the Search box, type "regedit", as shown in Figure 6.50, and press Enter. Regedit will appear at the top of the window. Double-click regedit to launch the program.

   If using the Windows Classic Start menu, you need to click on Run, enter "regedit", and click OK.

2. Navigate to the following folder, as demonstrated in Figure 6.51:

   HKEY_LOCAL_MACHINE\SOFTWARE\Microsoft\Windows\ CurrentVersion\Policies\System

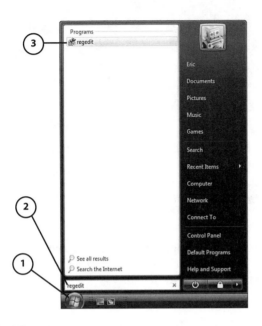

1. Open the Start Menu.

2. Type "regedit" in the Search box and press Enter.

3. Double-click regedit to launch the program.

FIGURE 6.50

Accessing the Registry Editor.

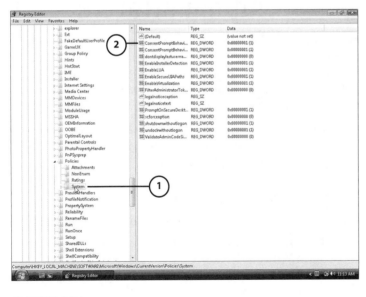

1. Navigate to HKEY_LOCAL_MACHINE\SOFTWARE\Microsoft\Windows\CurrentVersion\Policies\System.

2. Then, double-click ConsentPromptBehaviorAdmin.

FIGURE 6.51

Navigating to the System registry folder and opening the registry key properties.

3. In the right pane, double-click the following key:

   ConsentPromptBehaviorAdmin

4. In the Value Data field, type "0", as shown in Figure 6.52, and click OK.

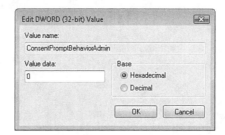

FIGURE 6.52

Inputting the new registry key value.

5. Now you can close the Registry Editor to apply the changes.

91 Use Computer Lock for Security When Leaving

Are you concerned about the security or privacy of your PC and its data? If so (and you should be), this tip is for you. As you might know, when you need to leave the computer, you can lock it so others can't use it without the password. Of course, you must have a Windows account password enabled for the locking feature to serve its purpose.

Here are a few ways you can lock your PC:

- Press Ctrl+Alt+Delete and click the Lock This Computer button (which was also in Windows XP), as shown in Figure 6.53.
- Use the new Lock option on the Start menu, as shown in Figure 6.54.
- If you're good with keyboard shortcuts, there's another quick way to lock your PC. Just press the Windows logo key+L and your PC will be instantly locked, which also works in Windows XP.

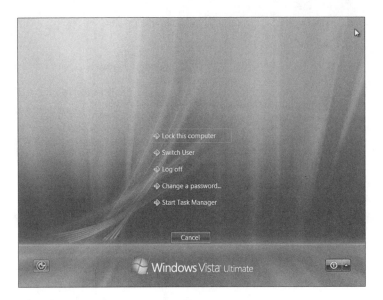

FIGURE 6.53

Locking your PC.

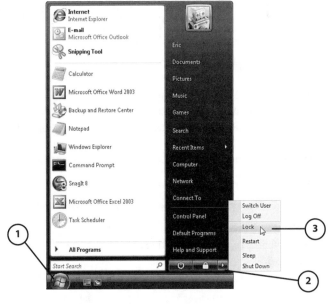

FIGURE 6.54

Using the Lock option.

(1) Choose Start.

(2) Click the arrow on the bottom right of the Start menu.

(3) Choose Lock.

 TIP

The next topic shows how you can add a shortcut to your desktop and/or the Quick Launch toolbar that will lock your computer.

92 Create a Shortcut to Lock Your Computer

As discussed in the previous tip, you can lock your PC (when using a password-protected Windows account) to provide security when leaving your desk. In addition to the ways already discussed in the previous tip, you can add a shortcut to your desktop and/or the Quick Launch toolbar to have another option at your fingertips when locking your PC:

1. Right-click on the desktop, point to New, and then click Shortcut.

2. In the location field, enter the following (Figure 6.55 shows an example):

   rundll32.exe user32.dll, LockWorkStation

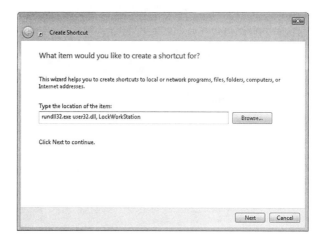

FIGURE 6.55

Entering a shortcut location.

3. After clicking Next, enter a name for the shortcut and click Finish.

4. For even quicker access to the Lock shortcut, you can add the icon to the Quick Launch toolbar. Just drag the new desktop icon and drop it into the Quick Launch area.

93 Auto-Login to Bypass the Logon Screen

If you have multiple user accounts on your PC but you're the main user, you might want to enable auto-login. That way, you don't have to click your account icon on the logon screen each time the PC is booted up. Then, if you need to access the other accounts, you can choose Switch User from your account to access the logon screen.

Here's how to enable auto-login:

1. Open the Start Menu, type "netplwiz," and press Enter.

   If using the Windows Classic Start menu, you need to click on Run, enter "netplwiz", and click OK.

2. Uncheck the Users Must Enter a User Name and Password to Use This Computer option, as shown in Figure 6.56.

 CAUTION

Keep in mind that enabling auto-login for accounts that use password protection defeats the idea of the protection it provides. Someone can just boot up the PC and it will automatically load into your password-protected account. It's best to use the auto-login feature if you aren't worried about others getting into your account.

FIGURE 6.56

Enabling auto-login.

① Choose the user account you want to allow to log on automatically.

② Select Users Must Enter a User Name and Password to Use This Computer.

3. Click Apply.

4. In the Automatically Log On window, enter the username and password (twice) for the account you want to auto-login, and click OK.

5. Click OK to exit.

94 Change Windows Using Flip 3D

In XP, switching between applications with the Alt+Tab key combination was a neat trick, but you should check out Flip 3D, new in Vista, which allows you to see a small thumbnail of each application as you cycle through them.

As Figure 6.57 shows, the new Flip 3D feature provides a much better image of the currently open applications/windows. It's actually a live thumbnail, so you can see the current state of the application/window.

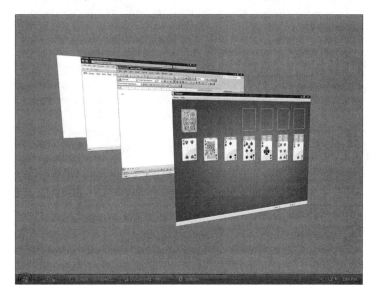

FIGURE 6.57

Example of the new Flip 3D feature.

To bring up Flip 3D, simply press the Windows logo key+Tab. Keep pressing the Tab key (while holding the Windows logo key) to cycle through the applications/windows. After you see the application/window you want, just release the Windows logo key and the selected window/application will fly into position.

You can also flip through the applications/windows with the arrows on the keyboard or the scrolling wheel (if you have one) on your mouse. Choose whatever works best for you.

95 Add Providers to Live Search in Internet Explorer 7

You might have noticed the new Live Search feature added to Microsoft Internet Explorer 7, which gives you quick access for your web searching needs. By default, the Search box uses Microsoft Live Search; however, you can add other search engines such as Google or Yahoo!, and even topic-related sites such as Amazon, Monster, or eBay. If the site you're looking for isn't already on the list, you can manually add it, which allows you to use just about any website with searching capabilities.

After you've added search engines to the list, you can specify one of the sites for the default that's searched when you simply type something in the field and press Enter (or click the Search button). Then to search the other sites, you type something in the field, click the arrow, and select the site you want to search, as shown in Figure 6.58. This is why the new searching feature is so great—you have many search engines and web-sites to search from by just a few clicks of the mouse!

FIGURE 6.58

Example of using Live Search with multiple providers.

Here's how to add providers to the Instant Search box in Internet Explorer 7:

1. In Internet Explorer, click the arrow next to the Search box and select the Find More Providers option. A web page appears, such as that shown in Figure 6.59.

FIGURE 6.59

Example of web page to add providers to Live Search.

2. Simply click on a site to add it to the Instant Search box, or manually add it by following the directions in the Create Your Own section. You'll be prompted to confirm that you want to add the site. Click Add Provider.

3. If you want to make the search engine or website your default search provider, check the appropriate check box.

4. Click the Add Provider button to proceed.

96 Change the Home Page of New Tabs in Internet Explorer 7

By default in Internet Explorer, you are prompted with the Welcome to Tabbed Browsing page when clicking on a new tab. However, this might be slightly annoying and you might wonder why it doesn't just open your defined home page instead.

Well, good news, you can easily make new tabs go to your start page:

1. Open Internet Explorer 7.

2. Click on Tools on the menu bar and select Internet Options.

3. Click the Settings button in the Tabs section, as shown in Figure 6.60.

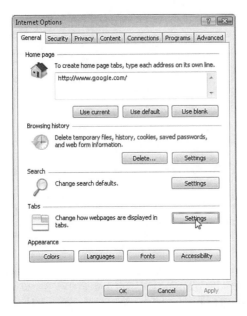

FIGURE 6.60

Opening the tabs settings.

4. Check the Open Home Page for New Tabs Instead of a Blank Page option, as pointed out in Figure 6.61.

5. Click OK.

Now that you fixed that issue, there's something even better: You can set multiple home pages to open in different tabs each time you start your browser. Like many other web users, you likely have more than one favorite website. Here's the solution to this dilemma:

1. Open Internet Explorer 7.

2. Click Tools on the menu bar and select Internet Options.

3. In the Home Page box, enter your desired website addresses. See Figure 6.62 for an example.

4. Click OK.

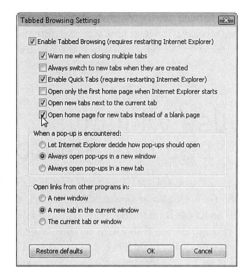

FIGURE 6.61

Making blank tabs open to your home page.

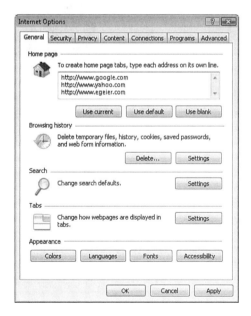

FIGURE 6.62

Entering home pages for tabs.

To see the changes, you must first close and reopen any currently open web browsers. The next time you open Internet Explorer, it should automatically load tabs for each of the websites you just specified.

97 Use Windows Keyboard Shortcuts

Keyboard shortcuts are one of the biggest advantages "computer geeks" have over the average user. Unlike other computer tasks, keyboard shortcuts aren't self-learned, that is unless you go through a lot of trial and error. Using keyboard shortcuts can save a great deal of time. (I use many, with Ctrl C, V, and X being my most used, especially for this book!) Therefore, for your reference, Table 6.1 lists many common shortcuts. Some of the shortcuts shown in Table 6.1 are specific to Vista, whereas some worked in previous versions of Windows.

Table 6.1 Common Vista Keyboard Shortcuts

Action	Shortcut
Open or close the Start menu	Windows logo key
Show desktop	Windows logo key+D
Show Windows Sidebar and gadgets	Windows logo key+spacebar
Open Quick Launch shortcuts	Windows logo key+# (1, 2, 3, etc.)
Open Computer	Windows logo key+E
Open Windows Explorer	Windows logo key+E
Minimize all windows	Windows logo key+M
Restore minimized windows	Windows logo key+Shift+M
Change task selection on Taskbar	Windows logo key+T
Open Task switch	Alt+Tab
Open 3D Flip—Task switch	Windows logo key+Tab
Open the Run prompt	Windows logo key+R
Open Search tool	Windows logo key+F
Lock the PC	Windows logo key+L
Access the System properties	Windows logo key+Pause/Break
Prevent AutoPlay when a disc loads	Shift

TIP

A trick to learn more keyboard shortcuts is to look through the menus in any program and note the keyboard shortcuts to the right of each command.

Action	Shortcut
Run executable with elevated privileges	Ctrl+Shift+Enter
Perform the Copy function	Ctrl+C
Perform the Paste function	Ctrl+V
Perform the Cut function	Ctrl+X

98 Use the Snipping Tool to Capture Screenshots

Windows now includes software to capture screenshots, called the Snipping Tool. This tool allows you to save an image of your screen or a selected area or window. You can save the image in several different formats: PNG, GIF, JPEG, or MHT.

Those who have previously used the Print Screen button on their keyboard to capture screenshots will greatly appreciate this addition to Windows. It saves you from a tedious and crude process, which consists of pressing the Print Screen button to copy an image of your current screen to the Clipboard, pasting the image into an editor (such as Paint), and then manually cropping and manipulating the screenshot for the window or area you want to save.

Here's how to access and use the Snipping Tool:

1. Open the Start menu, and open the Snipping Tool by following this path:

   All Programs, Accessories, Snipping Tool

2. After you open the Snipping Tool, you'll automatically be in the capturing mode. You can move your cursor around to select a window and click to snip it. Hitting your Esc key will get you out of the capturing mode.

3. After you snip, a preview window will appear where you can make edits to the image and save it.

4. You can use other Snipping methods, such as a Full-screen capture, by clicking the New button's arrow on the Snipping Tool. After you're ready to capture images, click the New button.

5. Remember, you configure additional settings by clicking the Options button on the Snipping Tool.

99 Adjust Audio Levels per Application

A new feature of Vista, not in prior versions of Windows, allows you to control the audio levels for some individual applications. This can be especially useful if you have a desk job and boredom has struck. Now you can play games with the volume down, while still hearing other sounds such as from your work applications; so it sounds like you're working!

To adjust the audio levels for individual applications, you use the Volume Mixer:

1. Double-click on the Volume icon in the system tray.

2. Click the Mixer link, as shown in Figure 6.63. The Volume Mixer dialog box opens.

3. Adjust the volumes using the slider bar.

FIGURE 6.63

Opening the Volume Mixer.

100 Use the Sync Center

Windows Vista comes with a new program, called Sync Center, to help you synchronize files between supported mobile devices and your computer. Many mobile devices support this type of synchronization, such as portable music (MP3) players, digital cameras, mobile phones, and USB flash drives. In addition, Vista Business and Ultimate editions also allow synchronization of files and folders on network drives.

Here's how to set up a device with Sync Center:

1. Plug the mobile device into your computer.

2. Install any software/drivers that came with the device.

3. Open the Start menu and open Sync Center by following this path:

   All Programs, Accessories, Sync Center

4. Click the Set Up New Sync Partnerships link, as pointed out in Figure 6.64, in the tasks pane on the left.

 TIP

The Windows Mobile Device and Sync Center in Vista takes the place of an older synchronization application you might have used before, called ActiveSync, with previous versions of Windows.

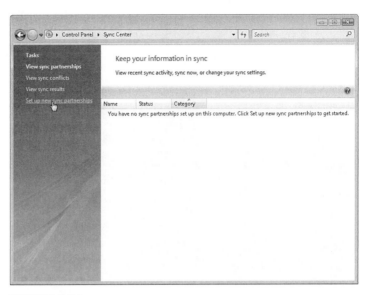

FIGURE 6.64

Starting the setup process of new Sync device.

 TIP

If the device doesn't appear on the list, it might not be supported for use with Sync Center. You should check the device manufacturer's website for more information. You might have to use their software to sync or they might offer a driver to install that will enable support with Sync Center.

5. Double-click on the device you want to set up.

6. Follow the onscreen directions to set up the sync partnership.

Index